D0822629

Rescuing HEALTHCARE

In *Rescuing Healthcare*, co-authors Antony Bell and Dr. Denis Cortese achieve the astonishing feat of packing several thought-provoking books into one, all in the space of merely 264 pages. The book is part tutorial on the nature of transformational leadership, with insights and lessons that span organizational paradigms and circumstances. In addition, their book contains a searching critique of the philosophical, human, financial, and institutional foibles of our fragile and misguided healthcare system which has lost its way. The authors argue convincingly that by failing to place the well-being of patients at the heart of the enterprise, our system befuddles, frustrates, and even frightens those it ostensibly is designed to serve. In their most telling criticism, Bell and Cortese contend that our system is woefully shortsighted because it concentrates principally on treating patients' illnesses instead of preventing medical problems and keeping people healthy. *Rescuing Healthcare* could become a game-changer by inspiring a generation of transformational leaders—providers, payers, policymakers and patients alike—with the vision, courage, savvy and resolve to create a 21st century system truly devoted to the health of the American people.

—**Hugh B. Price**, former President and CEO of the National Urban League, former visiting professor in the Woodrow Wilson School at Princeton University, former non-resident senior fellow at the Brookings Institution

We need a health revolution to provide people with better outcomes, with greater convenience, at lower cost. Rescuing healthcare will take leadership and bold thinking—exactly what this book provides.

—**Steve Case**, Co-founder of AOL & Chairman of Revolution & The Case Foundation

Getting more for our health care dollars should be one of the nation's highest priorities, with credible estimates suggesting that we spend as much as 5 percent of our gross domestic product on health care that doesn't improve outcomes. And yet, in some sense, we already know how to attack this problem: as Cortese and Bell emphasize in this well-written book, some healthcare systems already do it. The problem is that such high-quality, high-value care is scattered and it needs to be universal, which in turn requires the leadership called for by Cortese and Bell. You may not agree with everything in this book, but it's important to read if you care about the healthcare your family receives and the economic and fiscal future of the United States.

—**Peter R. Orszag**, former Director of
the Office of Management and Budget

One of America's most eminent medical executives and a highly-regarded thought leader in leadership have given us a masterful overview of healthcare leadership and how to improve it. *Rescuing Healthcare* gets straight to the point, with a sharp diagnosis of our ills and a clear vision of where healthcare needs to go. Drawing on a lifetime of experience, Dr. Cortese and Antony Bell offer a detailed strategy to unite your organization around a common purpose, improve patient care, and succeed in a value-based environment.

—**Toby Cosgrove, MD**, CEO and President, Cleveland Clinic

Bell and Cortese clearly articulate the central importance of leadership to achieving high value, patient-centric health and wellness, as well as why it is so difficult, in the complex adaptive system of healthcare delivery. A compelling read for anyone who hopes to contribute to and experience the transformation of the US system of healthcare delivery.

—**William B. Rouse, Ph.D.**, Alexander Crombie Humphreys
Chair of Economics of Engineering, Stevens Institute of Technology;
Member, National Academy of Engineering; Author, *Understanding
and Managing the Complexity of Healthcare* (MIT Press)

Bell and Cortese describe the symptoms of our health system in distress. They then lay out the leadership traits that are required to change our healthcare system. They make a convincing case that without leadership we cannot transform our healthcare system. They go on to describe the tangible and intangible assets that make for a transformational leader. This is a must read for all current and aspiring leaders in healthcare.

—**Michael M. E. Johns MD**, Executive Vice President for Health Affairs,
President/CEO and Chair Emory Healthcare Emeritus; Professor, Schools of
Medicine and Public Health; former Dean, Johns Hopkins School of Medicine

Rescuing Healthcare is essential reading for anyone involved in health care reform, be it as a provider, payer or governmental body. Good ideas as well as practices will only flourish when leadership and dedication reinforce one another. This is the great lesson from this wonderful book.

—**Ab Klink**, former Dutch Minister of Health, Welfare and Sport (2006-2010); Professor at the Free University Amsterdam

Rescuing Healthcare is a provocative, inspiring, and ultimately hopeful, call to action. Denis Cortese and Tony Bell effectively deploy equal parts moral suasion and a kick in the seat of the pants to make the case that the vision of high-quality, affordable health care for everyone is within reach, but only if those on the frontlines of patient care step up and take charge of changing health care. We as patients can only hope the clinicians and providers we rely on will read it.

—**Nancy-Ann DeParle**, Founding Partner, Consonance Capital, and Former Deputy Chief of Staff for Policy to President Barack Obama

The uniqueness of *Rescuing Healthcare* is that it not only addresses healthcare's profound problems from a leadership perspective, but it also spells out the kind of leadership it will take to reverse its self-destructive direction. A must-read for anyone involved in healthcare—as we all are.

—**Jim Barksdale**, Former President & CEO Netscape; Former COO, CEO AT&T Wireless; EVP and COO Federal Express; Chairman and President of Barksdale Management Corporation

As the clock runs out on American health care, Denis Cortese and Antony Bell offer a provocative and uniquely American solution to its failings: bold leadership. They tell policymakers, managers, clinicians and the public to step up to the plate and take on the challenges in the industry before it is too late. They show vivid examples of how strong leadership has improved quality, reduced waste and made medical treatments a livable experience. No one can read this book without believing that we can tackle these problems and must do it now.

—**David J. Brailer, MD** PhD, CEO Health Evolution

In *Rescuing Healthcare*, Antony Bell and Denis Cortese argue that we can move to a system of care that is truly efficient, effective, and affordable—but only if those who actually deliver the care take the lead in developing solutions that work. This is no fairy tale—it is already happening in communities across the country where health leaders work together to find ways to improve care and cut cost for the system as a whole. Bell and Cortese make a persuasive case that the health sector can save itself, but to do so will take leaders who are willing to collaborate in developing solutions that provide the greatest value to patients. This important and useful book will remind everyone that collaboration is more likely to lead to solutions than confrontation—and that's a particularly important lesson in this day and age.

—**Joe Antos Ph.D.**, Wilson H. Taylor Scholar in Health Care and Retirement Policy, American Enterprise Institute; Adjunct Associate Professor of Emergency Medicine, George Washington University

Antony Bell and Denis Cortese have presented a clear picture of what healthcare must become if it is to deliver better outcomes at affordable costs. They insist that we must redirect our attention to the well-being of patients from our present fixation on the interests of providers and payers now served by fee for service medicine. They describe the qualities of leadership necessary if we are to change direction, and they inspire us to exercise such leadership. Bell and Cortese have given us a guidepost pointing the way to what must and will be the future of healthcare.

—**John Danforth**, Former US Senator

Antony Bell and Denis Cortese, have written a book that is both important, inspiring and based in reality. At a time when physicians and providers are struggling to retain their mission and purpose, in an increasingly dysfunctional health care system, *Rescuing Healthcare* is a call to action and a manifesto for positive change, driven by those on the front lines, the ones actually making the decisions that affect patients' lives every day. This is a must read for anyone interested in health care improvement, from those entering medical school to seasoned physicians, administrators, and policymakers.

—**Dr. James N. Weinstein**, DO, President/CEO Dartmouth-Hitchcock Health; Peggy Y. Thomson Professor in the Evaluative Clinical Sciences, Geisel School of Medicine at Dartmouth and The Dartmouth Institute for Health Policy and Clinical Practice

Antony Bell and Denis Cortese have partnered to produce a remarkably accessible and insightful book on one of the nation's thorniest and most compelling challenges: our dysfunctional health care system. Despite our position as far and away the international leader in health expenditures—some 50 percent higher than the country ranked as the #2—we rank well down the quality list, behind at least 30 other countries according to the World Health Organization. Drawing on their complementary blend of deep experience shaping leadership for complex circumstances, Bell and Cortese lay out the prerequisites for progress, founded in a continuously learning system, in which the incentives are focused on patients and the outcomes they deserve. At the same time, in a sobering nod to reality, they liken the courage, will, and leadership required to that of the D-Day battlefields. Such is the nature of optimism when it comes to health care today.

—**J. Michael McGinnis MD MPP**, National Academy of Medicine Leonard D. Schaeffer Executive Officer

The combined experience of a leadership development guru and a uniquely significant healthcare leader led to the impressively titled and written *Rescuing Healthcare*. Healthcare is too important to leave in the hands of policy makers, providers and insurers. Antony Bell and Dr. Denis Cortese provide the rationale and understanding for all of us to play our part in leading the necessary change in healthcare. It is an exciting thesis and a great read.

—**Gary Bisbee, Jr., Ph.D.**, MBA, Chairman and CEO, The Health Management Academy

Today we live in a very complex world where no one, neither an institution, a government nor a country can operate on its own. This also applies in particular to the healthcare environment. As explained in this book, more than ever vision combined with strong leadership, ownership and execution power are needed. The role of leadership gets the special focus it deserves. It has led to an impressive unique workout. The parallel with D-day is daring, but extremely inspiring and convincing. Born in World War II and having enjoyed for so many years the success of the victory, I sincerely wish that this book will contribute in the same spirit to find real solutions for the huge healthcare challenges we are facing nowadays. That is why I strongly recommend reading it.

—**Henk van den Breemen**, General RNLMC retired, former CHOD NL

Rescuing Healthcare provides an excellent overview of the journey that has produced the current crisis in American healthcare. The authors also present an effective framework for understanding the need to transform American healthcare, the complexity of the task and the central role that leadership occupies in accomplishing the shift from volume to value. The format of the book will facilitate the thoughtful dialogue that will be essential to the creation of a sustainable system for creating a person-centric system for delivering health care, service, support and information.

—**Charles Barnett**, former CEO, Chairman of the Board Seaton Ascension

This wonderful book links a clear explanation of why health care is failing to a compelling prescription for change. There is no question that lack of leadership is at the heart of the many problems we face. Who can rescue health care? With the insights and guidance of this book, we all can.

—**Elliott S. Fisher, MD**, MPH, John E. Wennberg Distinguished Professor, Geisel School of Medicine at Dartmouth; Director, The Dartmouth Institute for Health Policy and Clinical Practice

Healthcare is at a critical junction. While technological, biological, and analytic capabilities hold great promise there are unprecedented opportunities for visionary leaders to step forward and create health systems that are truly focused on the people they serve by preventing illness and injury whenever possible, restoring optimal health when possible, and provide meaningful support through transitions when healing isn't possible. The nation's health and financial stability will depend on leaders who understand and apply leadership skills to navigate the transition to patient-centered healthcare. In clear writing, Antony Bell and Denis Cortese bring considerable experience and wisdom to bear on the problems and possible solutions, and give insight into the leadership competencies needed to transform the delivery of healthcare.

—**Charles W. Sorenson, MD**, FACS, President and CEO Intermountain Healthcare

Bell and Cortese have teamed up in a unique way to share their distilled lifetime of experiences—Cortese with a deep understanding of the complexities of our healthcare system, and Bell with a remarkable leadership framework that is essential for real change. The combination is a perfect recipe for genuinely transformational leadership within healthcare. While their writing is simple to comprehend, it makes a powerful appeal for the discipline, courage, and commitment it will take to rescue healthcare. An essential book for its resuscitation.

—**Gary Strack**, Executive Mentor Merryck & Co.,
Former President/CEO Orlando Regional Healthcare System

Health care in this country is on the cusp of a golden age. Medical science gets better every day. The tool kits to support patient care are constantly improving. The technology to deliver complete information to each caregiver about each patient is better than it has ever been, and that functionality is going to improve to the point where physicians and caregivers will have the ability to act on full information in real time about each of the patients they serve.

All of that functionality has the potential to be transformational and to create a truly golden age for patient care. But that transformation will not happen unless someone leads it. Care will not serendipitously organize itself. Care systems will not spontaneously emerge and function as systems. Transformation will not happen on its own. It needs to be organized. It needs to be led.

Leaders are the key. Health care needs leaders who have the vision, expertise and organizational skills to lead caregivers and health care organizations to that golden age.

This book is about those leaders. It's about leaders who truly improve and transform care, and the next levels of actualization for the new tool kit for care and the new science of care will only happen if leaders with vision do the right things to make them happen.

The authors are experienced and wise health care and business leaders with both insight and vision. They have given us the critical elements of leadership for the transformation of healthcare, and anyone who wants to see healthcare transformed should read this book—and support those leaders trying to get the job done in the ways that it needs to get done.

—**George C. Halvorson**, Chair and CEO Institute for Inter Group
Understanding; Retired Chair/CEO Kaiser Permanente Health System

Cortese and Bell have crafted an enlightened, thorough and readable primer on leadership—in healthcare and elsewhere. Both aspiring and established healthcare leaders will benefit from mastering the wise lessons it conveys.

—**David Blumenthal, M.D.**, M.P.P., President of The Commonwealth Fund

The delivery of higher quality in health care requires leadership as much or more than payment reform and new models of care. This very readable volume, by national experts, describes the key attributes of effective leadership and shows how they have driven value in successful health care organizations. This is essential reading for all health care stakeholders, especially emerging leaders.

—**John W Rowe M.D.**, Former CEO, Mount Sinai Health System and Aetna

Authors Antony Bell and Denis Cortese cut through the complexities of our healthcare crisis to provide health care professionals, policy makers and other stakeholders the right questions to ask, and refreshingly clear, convincing, and sensible answers that lead us toward much-needed transformation.

—**Mindy J. Fain, MD**. President,
American Academy of Home Care Medicine. Co-Director,
University of Arizona Center on Aging, President of AAHCM

Rescuing
HEALTHCARE

A Leadership Prescription
to Make Healthcare
What We All Want It to Be

ANTONY BELL
DENIS A CORTESE, MD

New York

Rescuing HEALTHCARE
A Leadership Prescription to Make Healthcare What We All Want It to Be

© 2017 **ANTONY BELL** and **DENIS A CORTESE, MD**

All rights reserved. No portion of this book may be reproduced, stored in a retrieval system, or transmitted in any form or by any means—electronic, mechanical, photocopy, recording, scanning, or other,—except for brief quotations in critical reviews or articles, without the prior written permission of the publisher.

Published in New York, New York, by Morgan James Publishing. Morgan James and The Entrepreneurial Publisher are trademarks of Morgan James, LLC.
www.MorganJamesPublishing.com

The Morgan James Speakers Group can bring authors to your live event. For more information or to book an event visit The Morgan James Speakers Group at www.TheMorganJamesSpeakersGroup.com.

Shelfie

A **free** eBook edition is available with the purchase of this print book.

CLEARLY PRINT YOUR NAME ABOVE IN UPPER CASE

Instructions to claim your free eBook edition:
1. Download the Shelfie app for Android or iOS
2. Write your name in **UPPER CASE** above
3. Use the Shelfie app to submit a photo
4. Download your eBook to any device

ISBN 978-1-68350-136-7 paperback
ISBN 978-1-68350-137-4 eBook
ISBN 978-1-68350-138-1 hardcover
Library of Congress Control Number:
2016910005

Cover Design by:
Rachel Lopez
www.r2cdesign.com

Interior Design by:
Bonnie Bushman
The Whole Caboodle Graphic Design

In an effort to support local communities, raise awareness and funds, Morgan James Publishing donates a percentage of all book sales for the life of each book to Habitat for Humanity Peninsula and Greater Williamsburg.

Get involved today! Visit
www.MorganJamesBuilds.com

Dedication

This book is dedicated to those of us who are patients now and to those who will be in the future ... which means it's dedicated to everyone—our readers and non-readers alike.

This book is also for our grandchildren—Connor and Zoe (Denis), and Drew, Ian and Benjamin (Antony), and for our children—Case and Holly (Denis), and Eric and Florence and her husband Andrew (Antony), with the hope that by the time they reach our age, the aberrations of the present healthcare system will be relegated to a footnote in history.

Table of Contents

Acknowledgement

No work of this kind is done alone. It rests on the shoulders of those who have thought and practiced before us and alongside us. Michael Porter has been a relentless promoter of the importance of "value" in healthcare delivery and has tirelessly raised its awareness at national and international leadership levels. And then there are those like Harvey Fineberg and Michael McGinnis who had the courage to launch the National Academy of Medicine's (formerly the Institute of Medicine) Round Table on Value and Science-Driven Healthcare. We describe others like them in the final chapter of this book, and we acknowledge their profound contribution and the example they set. Other great thinkers, such as Peter Senge with his work on systems thinking (and his description of a "learning organization" which has fundamental parallels for healthcare), and others such as Jim Collins, John Kotter and Ram Charan—these have all stretched and challenged our thinking, even if we haven't always agreed with them. We are indebted to them and to many others whom we do not have the space to mention.

And then there are those we work with and live with, who have bolstered this work by their comments and contributions. Natalie Landman not only contributed with the practical formatting of its images and diagrams, but she provided a very substantive contribution through her research on the last chapter and editorial advice on several chapters. Robert K. Smoldt gave us dedicated and unselfish assistance throughout the book. For me (Denis) Bob has always provided unwavering leadership and relentless support for improving the care of patients. Gary Strack provided valuable insights, and for me (Antony) has been a long-time friend and collaborator in the promotion of great leadership. In addition, as authors, we both owe many thanks to the colleagues of many years for their expertise, advice, and mentoring. For Antony, friends and colleagues like Dan Shoultz, Leslie and Matt Martin, Ed Walker, and Mark Bolte have been and are invaluable. For Denis, many thanks to friends and colleagues including Michael Crow, Eric Edell, Michael Joyner, Jack Leventhal, Margo Peters, Leslie and Matt Martin, Franklyn Prendergast, Robert Rizza, Donald Robinson, Nina Schwenk, Stephen Swensen, Victor Trastek, and Robert Waller.

Please do not hold all of those we have mentioned accountable for our points of view and the content. The responsibility for any disagreement with any of the content rests squarely on us as authors.

We are also indebted to our publisher Morgan James—to Margo Toulouse, David Hancock, Jim Howard, Nickcole Watkins, to mention but some; they are a pleasure to work with. We are also grateful to Justin Spizman for his editorial contribution.

Finally, this book would not have been possible without the patience, support and encouragement of our wives Donna (Denis) and Betsy (Antony). They have listened and provided a critical sounding board for all our work. We thank them for their unwavering encouragement.

Asking the Right Questions

"We are not getting what we are paying for."
Presidents, Politicians, and the Public

Healthcare is in trouble. Serious trouble.

In Ernest Hemingway's novel *The Sun Also Rises*, one of the characters asks another, "How did you go bankrupt?" "Two ways," came the reply. "First gradually, then suddenly."

However close healthcare is to bankruptcy, it's heading in that direction. For many, it's uncomfortably close, and when it comes, we will be as bankrupt as Hemingway's hapless character.

Healthcare is not just in trouble; it's in crisis—a self-generating crisis with a life of its own. It's on a troubling path, and it raises troubling questions.

The Questions We All Ask

The chances are you have your own questions about healthcare. You most likely discuss them with friends and debate them with colleagues. They may even keep

xix

you awake at night. Healthcare impacts us all. Whether you pay your own way or rely on third-party support, living a life without proper healthcare is a dangerous game of Russian roulette we all want to avoid. And because of the pressing need to avoid it, we tend to equate healthcare with healthcare *insurance*—something the press does and that we all do. But the issues of healthcare are much more than just about healthcare insurance; they are really about healthcare *delivery*. The fact is that we can have excellent coverage and still get horrible treatment—just look at the huge variability in healthcare delivery for people on Medicare, despite the fact that they all have coverage.

Healthcare is complex and confusing, and it's far bigger than who pays for it. This book takes us far beyond the debate over coverage. It takes us to the heart of the healthcare crisis—to healthcare *delivery*. And it also takes us to the source of its solution—the kind of *leadership* that will lead us out of the crisis. And it does much more: it defines *who* should provide that leadership … and *how!*

So let's dive into some of the most important questions that we most frequently ask—and that trouble us the most.

Question #1: Is healthcare really in trouble?
Yes. And here is why. Healthcare is crippled by the incapacity to deliver high-value healthcare on a universal scale. In some parts of the country, we see extraordinary examples of people receiving high-value care, but the vast majority of the United States does not. The extreme variations in patient-care outcomes, in safety, and in service are huge and often inexplicable. For the vast majority of the population, healthcare comes with poor patient focus, untimely care, and is delivered in the wrong location—and offered at astronomical levels of national spending. As a nation, we suffer from low-value healthcare, we do not receive uniformly high-value healthcare, and we do not get what we are paying for. Healthcare is in trouble for other reasons as well, and we will explore them in later chapters.

Question #2: Won't health insurance for all solve the problem?
No. Universal health insurance will simply provide greater access to an inefficient system. Insurance does nothing to improve healthcare delivery itself.

As mentioned before, people with insurance (employer-based, commercial insurance, Medicare, Medicaid, TriCare, VA insurance, the Federal Employees Health Benefit Plan, Indian Health Service) are the very same people receiving the delivery of healthcare of highly variable quality, outcomes, safety, and service—at very high costs. The simple presence of insurance has not resolved the problem of low-value healthcare in the USA.

Question #3: What should the country expect?
As a nation, we need and should expect a high-value healthcare system—with better outcomes, better safety, and better service, all wrapped up with lower levels of spending. In addition, we should expect a *learning* system in an environment where everyone in the healthcare system knows what the healthcare system knows. There is little, if any, transparency within the entire healthcare system in terms of outcomes, safety, service, pricing, and insurance. Think of the last time you renewed or even changed your healthcare insurance. Was it easy? Did you understand your policy? In all likelihood, you felt exactly the same way most Americans feel when they interact with the healthcare system: uninformed and overwhelmed. By what exactly? Complex insurance, lack of transparency between the providers and the patient, lack of medical records interoperability, lack of a caring and compassionate "primary" doctor, poor care in hospitals, unexplained duplication of tests, poor safety, complications and side effects, unnecessary surgery and other procedures, inability to get in touch with your provider when needed, and so on and so on. The least the healthcare delivery system can do is to improve outcomes, safety, and service—and lower the costs.

Question #4: What is the financial imperative?
If unresolved, healthcare will become economically crippling. The unfunded liabilities for Medicare and Medicaid alone are a serious threat to economic growth and global competitiveness. The various estimates from the Institute of Medicine (now the National Academy of Medicine), economists, and healthcare delivery experts estimate that of the $3 trillion spent on healthcare delivery, a range from as low as 17 percent to as high as 50 percent is wasted in the healthcare system due to poor outcomes, complications, unnecessary tests, imaging, procedures,

medications, ineffective care, inefficient care, and untimely care, which is not patient-centered. The size of the actual number is not that important—what is important is the fact that waste is substantial.

Question #5: What is the urgency to get this done?
We are in a state of emergency. Before we know it, our otherwise fragile system will completely crumble around us. This may initially sound like an overstatement, but we'll make the case to support it in upcoming chapters. It is imperative to create a high-value healthcare system as soon as possible. The urgency is growing by the day. It is crucial to implement such a system before mainstream medical practice is submerged and battered by the impending tsunami of personalized medicine, genomics, proteomics, big data, and cloud-based gene warehouses—with the expensive novel diagnostic tests and individually tailored therapeutics that will inevitably accompany them.

Question #6: Do we have a solution to this overwhelming problem?
Absolutely. The best high-value providers around the country have figured out how to make it work. There is much we can learn from them.

Our challenge is less about knowing and more about doing. It's about getting going, as Gordon Bok told us in his old folk song, *Old Fat Boat*:

> "Mercy, Mercy
> I do declare,
> Half the fun of going
> Is the getting there.
> But Mercy Percy,
> You better start rowing,
> Cause the other half of getting there
> Is going!"

Now is the time to start rowing. At a national level, there is a convergence and momentum that hasn't existed in the past, but now the problems have reached a level of magnitude and we can no longer pretend they don't exist. As

Churchill once said, "You can trust Americans to do the right thing … after trying everything else first!"

And just about "everything else" has in fact been tried: price controls, fee-for-service payments, relative value units, diagnostic related groups, Health Maintenance Organizations (HMOs), Pay-for-Performance (which sounds good, but in its current form is actually pay-for-*compliance*), Group Practice Demonstration projects, Pioneer Accountable Care Organizations (ACOs), shared savings ACOs, evaluation & management coding requirements, International Statistical Classification of Diseases and Related Health Problems number 9 (ICD9 with ICD10 and ICD 11 on the way), Department of Justice coding and billing investigations, Recovery Audit Contractor audits—and others we may be missing.

Despite these initiatives, we are no further advanced. In fact, it is *because of* these initiatives that we are no closer to patient-centered, high-value healthcare on a national scale. These experiments in regulatory micromanagement have brought us to where we are today. So the time is right to try paying for what we say we want, and at the very least to link payments to better results with lower costs.

And this leads us to one unanswered question, the most important question of all …

Who Will Do This?

This is the critical question: *Who will provide the leadership to resolve this crisis?* It's the big-picture question. The problem is not that the crisis is insoluble. The problem is that we focus on the wrong question. The most important question is not *what* should we do, but rather, *who* should do it. If we can answer the *who* question, the *what* question will take care of itself—because the right leaders in the right places will know how to take care of it.

As Jerry Garcia put it in 1988 when he was trying to save his band, "Somebody has got to do something. It is just incredibly pathetic it has to be us!" So who is the "us?" It is the providers, those people who actually deliver healthcare. The folks who can change the way healthcare is delivered are those who actually deliver it. Their teams are on the front lines with the patient and the patient's family. *They* control clinical practice patterns and styles. *They* hold the key to unlock the door to resolution.

What do we mean by "providers"? We use a broad definition that includes doctors, nurses, pharmacists, nurse practitioners, physician assistants, systems and process engineers, health evaluation researchers, technical and allied health staff, health system administrators, architects, and financial planners ... in other words, those who directly deliver healthcare and those who support them.

Who else is "us"? It is also all those who support those on the front lines—the many who make their lives either easier or harder. We will explain who they are later.

But you still may be thinking: *Who* will lead the transformation of the healthcare delivery? The answer is this: the right leaders in the right places, exercising the right leadership in the role they fill. *That* is the most critical issue in healthcare.

And that is the focus of this book.

D-Day and Healthcare

D-Day was an extraordinary victory for one primary reason: the right people in the right places exercised the right leadership at the right time. Those who planned the strategy didn't directly train those who executed the strategy. Or in other words, the trainers didn't develop the strategy, and they didn't execute the strategy.

Those who executed the strategy—the soldiers who landed on the beaches—were given the freedom to adjust to circumstances that no amount of planning and training could ever anticipate. They could handle this freedom because they clearly understood the goals and the strategic objectives.

Whatever their role, all the leaders involved understood the scope of their leadership and led within that scope. That is what made D-Day such an overwhelming success.

Healthcare delivery today is far more complex and extensive than even D-Day. But the principles these wartime leaders applied should not be lost on us: just as D-Day succeeded because the right leadership was exercised by the right people in the right places, healthcare delivery today can enjoy an equal measure of success if the right leadership is applied by the right people in the right places.

What did that look like for D-Day? The senior leadership articulated a clear vision, defined the enemy, sold the message, and aligned the stakeholders. The next layer of leadership planned and organized the tactics, and most importantly, trained the troops, picking the best people to get the job done. They provided the skills and technology. The troops, in turn, performed well because they were prepared well.

With this in mind, consider the parallels between the two:

	D-Day	Healthcare
Defining the Purpose	• Win the war in Europe	• Provide high-value healthcare, and get what we are paying for
Clarifying the Enemy	• The German leaders and their forces	• Inefficiency in healthcare delivery (which results in variable outcomes, low safety, non-uniform service, and high costs) • Providers are not the enemy, as some suggest
Fighting on the Frontline	• The Allied troops	• The healthcare providers, as we defined them earlier
Leading at the Organizational Level	• The US President set the purpose of the mission • The Supreme Commander set the vision, developed the internal alignment, selected the operational leaders, and convinced the troops	• The US president and political leaders should set the mission for high-value care • The senior leaders in healthcare should carry it forward into their organizations

Leading at the Operational Level	• The senior staff under the command of the supreme commander worked collaboratively as a team, which included all the branches of the armed services of several countries. • They developed the plan for implementation including the resources, logistic support, skills training, culture development, top-level troop selection, and articulated the goals, objectives, and targets. • And very importantly, they remained fully engaged and responsible for all the ongoing logistical support (transportation, information, arms, food, fuel, and other resources). • Politicians and lobbyists did not interfere with the work of the troops, but they held the military leaders responsible for success.	• Once the mission and vision is clear, providers in senior leadership and operational leaders should carry the vision forward and clearly communicate it to their staff; they then should work to develop the culture, train the people, provide the tools, proceed with the planning, and be responsible for the implementation. • Politicians, lobbyists, and regulators should not interfere with the work of the providers, but they should hold provider leaders responsible for success.

Not that we are saying that healthcare reform is similar to war. But the intricacies and strategies needed to succeed are strikingly similar. The challenge we describe in this book is not saving Europe; it's saving healthcare. The mission in healthcare is to get better healthcare delivery and improved health for the money we spend. At this point, the value is not apparent and the result is a substantial waste of resources, to include both time and money.

D-Day would have been an unmitigated fiasco without senior leadership. Eisenhower would have had to send the letter he had prepared in case of failure: "The troops, the air and the Navy," he wrote, "did all that Bravery and devotion to duty could do. If any blame or fault attaches to the attempt it is mine alone." A sign of a true leader, he was prepared to take real personal responsibility if the operation failed. Thankfully, he never had to send that letter because the D-Day leaders exercised the right kind of leadership in the right roles at the right time, which produced spectacular outcomes.

Unfortunately, we cannot make the same claim in our current world of healthcare. We are making the mistakes that the leaders of D-Day avoided. Those who should be exercising the right leadership are not exercising it. Those devising the strategy are trying to dictate its execution, even though they don't practice medicine, and those charged with the execution don't understand how to lead the frontline transformation that only they can lead—partly because they do not own the vision, and partly because they are ill-prepared to lead the change.

It is time for policy makers to define the right strategy and set the right goals. It is time for regulators to establish accountability, and for providers to lead the execution of those goals and provide the right kind of accountability in doing so. While providers are most needed to lead the transformation of healthcare delivery, an ever-expanding level of micromanagement from the very groups who say they want much greater efficiency is hampering that crucial outcome. Strategy and execution are blurred, and oversight is confused with micromanagement. Oversight is necessary; micromanagement is not.

To combat the real enemy—inefficiency—we need to provide the resources, freedom, and accountability to those who really can improve care and reduce costs. We need doctors, nurses, nurse practitioners, medical administrators, pharmacists, leaders of medical organizations, project managers, system engineers, and financial officers to work together to improve results and lower costs for the patient. They are the only ones who can viably and durably improve healthcare delivery. Why? Because, collectively, they are on the frontlines of delivery. They practice medicine; governments and insurers do not. If they don't rise to the challenge, reform efforts from elsewhere will be counterproductive at worst and meaningless at best.

So Where Do We Go From Here?

This book is written to enable leaders in healthcare to emulate the leaders of D-Day. Its goal is to encourage leaders, whatever their contribution to healthcare, to exercise the right kind of leadership in the right role. It is written to help policy makers lead through policy that empowers healthcare providers to lead the way to high-value healthcare through execution. It is written to help healthcare providers know what kind of leadership they need to exercise. And it is written to show every other stakeholder in healthcare how their leadership can help transform healthcare.

The existing confusion of leadership roles may explain the relatively narrow focus of recent efforts of healthcare reform—primarily on insurance reform and insurance coverage. This is an important provision, but it addresses only one among several components of a healthy healthcare delivery system. Not everyone agrees on what those components should be, but the Institute of Medicine has identified six aims for our healthcare system that few people contest:[1]

- Wider and equitable access to insurance
- Patient-centered delivery
- Safety
- Effectiveness
- Efficiency
- Timeliness

Healthcare legislation has focused primarily on the first. The other five components are firmly anchored in the realm of healthcare's delivery system, and more to the point, firmly in the hands of the teams of providers we identified above. If they exercise the right kind of leadership, it will not only transform

---

1   "*Crossing the Quality Chasm: a new health system for the 21st century,*" the Committee on Quality Healthcare in America, Institute of Medicine 2001, published by the National Academy of Sciences.

healthcare delivery—it will ultimately help transform healthcare in general. It is they who must take charge of changing healthcare.

The Complexity of Reform

But that's no easy task. Healthcare delivery in the United States is an enormously complex, self-organizing system. It has evolved over many years to its current bloated state by responding to incentives that most often optimized the self-interests of stakeholders and seldom advanced the interests of patients, which should be its greatest concern.

To change such a system requires much more than just legislative action. It requires systems-thinking leaders who advance a shared vision for patient-centered delivery, with better results and lower costs. At the heart of the crisis of healthcare is a crisis of efficiency, with a system that rewards the wrong people with the wrong incentives to produce the wrong results. And if there is anyone who can change it, it is the providers of healthcare. Flawed as it may be, the Affordable Care Act, which was signed into law in 2010, set in motion changes that Congress itself cannot reverse. If properly harnessed, these changes will drive the transformation we all want to see in the delivery of healthcare, whatever other legislation may follow in its wake.

But that is not enough. It depends on those who deliver healthcare (both those directly involved with healthcare and those who support them). It depends on leaders at every level—not just those at the top of the organization—understanding how to lead within their spheres of influence to create and foster the environments that make change in healthcare delivery both possible and desirable. It depends on whether or not we are ready to be the conduits for change to create a better tomorrow.

The Power of Leadership

That is the purpose of this book: to define the kind of leadership it will take to profoundly and durably reform and transform the healthcare system.

It is written to equip those immersed in healthcare delivery with the tools and framework they need to fulfill the task that they are uniquely placed to fulfill. This book is for you—doctors, nurses, nurse practitioners, pharmacists, leaders of medical organizations, medical administrators, project managers, system engineers, and financial officers—you who come together to put on a virtuoso performance in healthcare delivery.

This book is also for those of you who train and educate healthcare providers. Every year, medical schools, nursing schools, and health administration colleges release a new wave of doctors, nurses, and administrators. But we wonder if each new wave of practitioners is prepared for the inexorable changes in healthcare and the kind of leadership these changes will need. The truth is that they may not be. And if they are not, then the behaviors and practices that created the problem will continue to perpetuate it.

Finally, this book is for legislators and policy makers—to help you recognize what you can do, and just as importantly, what you cannot do. This book is an appeal to you to support, rather than frustrate, the efforts of leaders who are the most willing and able to reform healthcare. We all need your support, as you are in a unique position to either create or remove obstacles and brick walls. With you, we can all tackle the challenges of healthcare with courage and strength. Without you, we may never recover.

And this book is for patients—present and future. That includes us all. At some time or another, we will all respectively rely on the healthcare industry to elongate or even save our lives. We don't want to think about it, but when there is a need, we surely better hope our health and livelihood is properly supported. We all have a vested interest in seeing the right people in the right role exercising the right leadership to lead the transformation of healthcare.

Is the Shift Even Possible?

Refocusing healthcare is a lofty goal. But it's an attainable goal if we address the two factors that make outstanding healthcare delivery elusive:

1. *The complexity of the current healthcare system itself*
2. *The confusion around leadership*

This book addresses the intersection of the confusion in healthcare and the confusion around leadership. It makes sense of the complexity of the healthcare environment, and it does so by focusing on what is essential for transforming healthcare delivery. At the same time, it makes sense of the complexity of leadership, and removes the mystery of great leadership. It is therefore a pragmatic book as it maps out a path to great leadership for anyone prepared to embark on the journey.

Mapping the Journey

Here is how we map out the path to accomplish our goals:

Part I defines the problem: the absence of leadership. In Chapter 1, we underscore the importance of leadership and why leadership is *the* critical variable in the success of any endeavor. Leadership, both good and bad, is contagious: leaders reproduce after their own kind. Its effects are also enduring, and linger on long after the leader has left.

In Chapter 2, we offer a short history of healthcare and the gradual erosion of the interests of the patient. In Chapter 3, we pinpoint the three major problems that beset healthcare and discuss why leadership is so important in resolving them.

In Chapter 4, we address the question of why leadership is so difficult in healthcare, and we discuss the dysfunctional relationship between the five domains of healthcare.

If the absence of leadership is the problem, and the answer is the presence of great leadership, we still need to define what direction that leadership needs to take us in … leadership, yes, but to what end?

That is the focus of Part II, and in Chapter 5, we start with the most profound of all questions, however obvious it may seem: why healthcare and what is its purpose? (The desirable answer is very different from the answer healthcare delivery currently operates by.) We then discuss the vision for healthcare (Chapter 6): what do we want healthcare delivery to look like in the future, and where do we want to take it? Only when we have addressed the purpose and vision for healthcare can we then address the third question for its transformation (addressed in Chapter 7): How should healthcare be organized to pursue its purpose and fulfill its vision? We discuss healthcare as a system, or a system of systems, and suggest how heath care delivery needs to be become a vibrant learning system. In the concluding chapter of Part II, we discuss culture and suggest three values that all stakeholders in healthcare can agree on, which can shape the way leadership is exercised in healthcare.

Part III addresses in detail the kind of leaders we need (and where we need them) for the transformation of healthcare. We define great leadership, and we offer a comprehensive framework that makes sense of the complexity of leadership. We ask the question of whether great leadership can actually be exercised in healthcare—a legitimate question. If the right people in the right places exercise the right kind of leadership in their respective roles, it certainly can. In Part III, we show what kind of leadership the key stakeholders need to exercise for us to see that happen.

Finally, in Part IV, we provide examples of organizations in healthcare that have exercised the kind of leadership we advocate and who are achieving the kinds of results our approach will yield. If by this stage you still have any traces of skepticism, Part IV will dispel them.

Back to Hemingway

Remember the Hemingway quote about going bankrupt? "First gradually, then suddenly." The good news about bankruptcy is that there is a gradual phase before the sudden phase. If the right steps are taken in the gradual phase, the sudden phase need never happen. Bankruptcy is far from inevitable.

But only if one critical condition is met: having the right leadership exercised by the right people in the right places.

Day in and day out, those on the frontlines of patient care need to exercise the right kind of leadership. And those whose decisions impact the way the frontline delivers care need to exercise the right kind of leadership. Only then will we avoid the sudden phase.

This book is a call to action for all those directly or indirectly involved in the extraordinarily difficult but immensely rewarding challenge of transforming healthcare. It's a call to exercise the kind of leadership that only you can offer in the particular contribution you make in shaping and directing the change we all want to see.

And to help you exercise that leadership, whatever your role, we provide you with the perspective and framework you need to help reshape the delivery world that every one of us encounters sooner or later—and one that, before long, we can be impressed by and grateful for.

PART I

The *Real* Problem: No Leadership!

When leaders stumble or crumble, their organizations stumble or crumble.

When organizations crumble, their sector stumbles.

When the sector stumbles, it's because those who should be leading fail to do so.

Leadership really matters.

For healthcare, no single topic deserves more attention than this.

Chapter 1

The Importance of Leadership

L eadership *matters*. It really matters. In every walk of life.

Whatever the challenge, endeavor, initiative, enterprise, time, age, field, context, or culture ... leadership is the critical variable that can often be viewed as the difference between success and failure. Whether it's in a hospital, in a company, in a non-profit organization, in politics, in government or in education, leadership is inevitably linked to the outcome of any situation. It is not the only variable, but it is the critical one.

Leaders stand on the fulcrum of events, and they tip the balance for either good or ill. They don't always create the events—but they always define the response.

So leadership matters. It mattered in the past, it matters today, and given the complexity of the world we lead in, it will matter more than ever in the future. Leadership matters because it is contagious. It matters because it is timeless. It matters to you personally. And it matters in healthcare.

Leadership Is Contagious

All leadership—good or bad—is contagious. It reproduces after its own kind. Lead with determination and dedication, and your team will follow with those same qualities. Provide scattered and undefined leadership, and your team will act in the same way. Your team doesn't just look to you to lead; it looks to how you lead.

With the power of a virulent epidemic, bad leadership begets bad behavior. Was Hitler alone in his abuses? Was Stalin alone in his? Of course not. They reproduced after their own kind; they attracted and shaped the kind of leaders who shared their aspirations. And by attracting the same kind of leaders, they shaped national behavior. Bad leadership begets bad behavior. Without other leaders who emulated their particularly ugly brand of leadership, Hitler and Stalin would most likely have been footnotes in history instead of the copious chapters that describe their gruesome legacies.

By the same token, good leadership begets good behavior. "Courage," Billy Graham once said, "is contagious. When a brave man takes a stand, the spines of others are often stiffened." In contrast to Hitler and Stalin, leaders like Washington, Adams, King Jr., Lincoln, and Mother Theresa attracted a very different kind of leader—with a very different kind of impact … just as extensive, but very different.

As in politics, so in any walk of human endeavor, including healthcare: leadership determines behavior. All leadership, good or bad, is contagious.

Leadership Is Timeless

Leadership matters because it is timeless. More accurately, it is not bound by the life of the leader who exercises it. We enjoy political freedoms today because over two hundred years ago, the founders of this nation set up a system of government to ensure the preservation of these liberties beyond their own lifetimes. Today, we still reap the benefits of their leadership. But in reality, we owe our freedoms not just to them, but also to those who came before them, because the leaders who preceded them influenced their leadership—a trickle-down effect of profound proportions. These eighteenth-century freedom fighters relied heavily on the framers of the 1689 Bill of Rights in England, who themselves relied on the example of those who drafted the 1215 Magna Carta, a document that firmly placed the monarch under the rule of law … not above it. But even they were not the ultimate source of our liberties. Their initiative was shaped by the example of someone who had lived more than 300 years before them: Alfred the Great, whose vision of a united England was at the heart of the creation of England as a nation state, and more importantly enshrined the notion of the nation's leaders being subject to the same laws as every other citizen. So here we are today, still feeling the impact of a leader who died more than eleven hundred years ago. Leadership does indeed outlast the life of the leader who exercises it. It is limitless, without boundaries, and never constrained by ceilings. It transcends time, barriers, and all that stands in its way.

And this is true for bad leadership as much as for great leadership. Should we be surprised that Russia produced a Stalin when Peter the Great set its patterns of leadership? Stalin far surpassed Peter the Great (a "great" of dubious merit) in the number of people killed or executed during his tenure (by some counts 60 million), but the difference was one of technology not intent. Stalin, incidentally, clearly understood the importance of leadership, which is why, at the outset of World War II when invading Poland as an ally to Hitler, he had over 20,000 Polish leaders, including 8,000 senior military officers, executed at what is now known as the Katyn Massacre. He understood there would be no resistance without the leaders to lead it.

When Jack Welch was asked about his greatest concern as he looked ahead to this present decade, his foremost concern was the absence of good leadership. Pulitzer Prize-winning author Thomas Friedman put it this way: "In this kind of world, leadership at every level of government and business matters more than ever. We have no margin of error anymore, no time for politics as usual or suboptimal legislation." Even the World Bank has weighed in when describing the economic woes of the Middle East and North Africa (Mena). It concluded that "at the root of Mena's growth gap is its governance gap" ("governance" is bureaucratic code for leadership).

Leadership Matters Personally

What does this mean for you? Well, for those of you we identified earlier—doctors, nurses, nurse practitioners, pharmacists, leaders of medical organizations, medical administrators, project managers, system engineers, and financial officers—you are those who now stand on the fulcrum of healthcare reform. The truth is that you can tip the scales in the direction of either good or bad. And whichever way you tip it, your leadership will far outlast your tenure. This, then, is a call to tip the force of events in the right direction. If you choose to, you have an opportunity to change the face of healthcare delivery.

Leadership is truly a personal matter. Think about how it matters for your career or your personal endeavors. Great careers are built on great leadership, not great expertise. A successful career is by definition a leadership career, even if you came into the marketplace with a specific functional expertise—whether in accounting, finance, law, marketing, engineering, or, of course, medicine. And personally, great leadership often takes form in thoughtful and meaningful parenting, where you educate and nurture the next generation of leaders into smart and compassionate young men and women. You may be a physician or a nurse, but gone are the days when your success was solely a function of your medical competence. The complexity of today's global economy has more than ever shifted leadership into the hands of functional experts, whose functional training has ill-prepared them for the leadership roles they are asked to embrace. But lack of preparation doesn't diminish the importance of leadership for you personally: more than ever, a successful healthcare career will be a leadership career.

Leadership Matters in Healthcare

Leadership matters, particularly in healthcare, and given the complexity of the healthcare system, it matters more than ever. Redefining healthcare as a well-functioning system—providing patient-focused, value-driven healthcare delivery—will not just happen by itself. It will happen because leaders like you choose to make it happen. Because when it comes right down to it, it is absolutely a choice. A choice just as much, and just as important, as the choice you made selecting your career path. It takes time and determination to become a great leader, but the journey of a thousand miles starts with a decision to put one foot in front of the other.

Consider that every question raised in seeking to develop a sound, healthy delivery system ultimately comes back to a leadership question. Notice the leadership implications of questions such as:

- How do we put the patient at the center of healthcare delivery?
- How do we create a delivery system based on value?
- Who are the people who can drive these profound shifts in healthcare delivery?
- How do we create a healthcare learning system?
- Who are the people who can drive the creation of this engineered system?
- Who are the most critical leaders who can most effectively implement it?
- What are the critical leadership functions they will need to implement it?

Whatever the best solution looks like, it remains an academic and esoteric exercise without the right kind of leadership to implement it. Many agree on the need to address healthcare as a systems issue; but few address the leadership it will take to create and implement it.

So leadership matters. Not just for healthcare in general, but also for your particular healthcare organization, whatever its size, scope, or purpose. Whether you are a physician, a nurse, a pharmacist, or a healthcare administrator, leadership is the one ingredient that more than any other will determine the success or failure of your organization. We tell the leaders we work with that the single most significant thing about an organization is what goes on in the minds of its leaders ... because what goes on in their minds will determine what they do as leaders, and what they do as leaders will shape the outcome of the enterprise they lead.

The undeniable importance of leadership begs another question: if leadership matters so much in healthcare, what are the problems they need to solve? That is the subject of our next chapter.

Chapter 2

A Short History of Healthcare
Losing Sight of the Customer

T o really understand the magnitude of the problem within the healthcare industry, we should turn back the clock and review the most substantial developments and historical events that created the broken foundation on which we rest. This brief history will likely show you just how deep the problem goes, and simultaneously help you understand why it seems so hard to dig out of this mess. Because of the size of the issue, a brief history will offer you the true magnitude of the problem. Only then can you truly see how desperately we need great leadership.

|||||||||||||||||||||||||||||||||||||||||||||||||||||||||||||||||||||||||||||||||||||||||||||||||||||||||||||||||||||||||||||||||||

The past is prologue, Shakespeare told us, and he was right: if we can understand the history of healthcare, we can understand why we are where we are. This chapter captures that history.

|||||||||||||||||||||||||||||||||||||||||||||||||||||||||||||||||||||||||||||||||||||||||||||||||||||||||||||||||||||||||||||||||||

The history of healthcare in America, and in much of the Western world, is a long history of one powerful trend: the displacement of the patient as the primary focal point. The patient is not the customer.

… At least not the *primary* customer. At best, the patient is *a* customer. The healthcare system is set up to put every other stakeholder ahead of the patient in its pecking order, and although many medical professionals fight to counter it, the system has a low view of the patient. The patient has been displaced. And that is a problem.

It is not an uncommon problem. We see it elsewhere, where customer interests are subjugated to supplier interests. A friend of mine (Antony), the CFO of a large discount distribution chain, explained how one very hot item—wicker baskets—was not moving from their stores, despite a huge interest and demand from customers. It turned out that the store managers were simply not displaying them because they were large, bulky, awkward to handle, and difficult to stack. Out of convenience, the managers were leaving them in the storage area. Whose interests were being served? Not the customers.

The same is true within the healthcare industry. The customer is not at the forefront of the service. The focal point of healthcare delivery now belongs to the providers and payers of healthcare. The patient is at their disposal. The current system is designed to serve the interests of medical healthcare providers, insurance companies, governments, employers, pharmaceutical and biotech companies, innovators and inventors (supported by taxpayer money and the Bayh-Dole Act), politicians (the more they give away, the more votes they get), lawyers, and consultants … but not those of the patient! The patient or the employee might still benefit from the delivery system, but the system is not designed to put them first. So they essentially come last.

We can't place all of the blame on healthcare providers (hospitals, physicians, and their supporting staff). We can justifiably argue that the patient has never been the focal point of healthcare, at least not since the days of agrarian America. But even if we acknowledge that at one time the patient was at the center, this centrality has progressively eroded since the introduction of both public and private health insurance.

There are, then, two sides to this coin: on one side, the patient; and on the other side, the remainder of the participants. Both contributed: patients lost sight of the cost and the rest lost sight of the patient. This created quite the vicious cycle. In both cases, third party payers drove the decisions. No longer having to pay directly for their own healthcare, patients wanted as much healthcare as possible, and with the patient no longer paying directly for healthcare delivery, the rest of the sector focused on those who did.

So, how did we get here? How did we lose a common purpose and a common vision, with the customer at the apex?

From One Huge Shift to Another

Over the last 150 years, the US economy has weathered two huge seismic macro-economic shifts. It moved first from a commodity-based economy to a mass-manufacturing economy, and then from a mass-manufacturing economy to an information-technology economy.

Even up to the Civil War, the American economy was a commodity-based economy (essentially an agricultural economy), and the vast majority of those who fought on both sides of the Civil War listed their professions as farmers.

All that changed with the Industrial Revolution, building up in the latter part of the nineteenth century, and gathering momentum in the early part of the twentieth century, until it evolved into a fully-fledged mass-manufacturing economy by the 1920s. Within a few years of the end of the First World War, the commodity-based economy was a thing of the past. The Second World War gave mass-manufacturing additional impetus, and the next decades saw it become a global phenomenon—at least in the industrialized West, driven by the abundance of relatively cheap energy.

The next major shift came in the early 1980s, with the advent of cheap microchips, and we moved rapidly and decisively into an economy driven by information technology. As information technology evolved, it transformed everything—from manufacturing to healthcare, and with it, the kind of social and economic transformations that we have witnessed over the past forty years.

From Healing Patients to Eliminating Disease

How did these macro-economic shifts affect the medical profession? When America was largely an agricultural society, healthcare was highly fragmented. Doctors were given some training (by the standards of the times, extensive training), but with the more rudimentary understanding of medicine at the time, they were pretty much left to their own devices. They operated independently, and they were very patient-focused. They had no other distractions, and they were for the most part altruistically driven. Being a doctor was a sacrificial commitment; there was little money to be made, though their contribution was revered and valued. As illustrated in the diagram below, the relationship between the doctor and the patient was straight forward, with plenty of discussion, not only on cures, but also on costs.

The Patient-Physician Relationship Before the Advent of the Payer

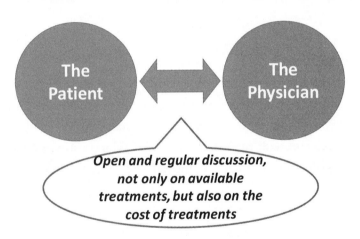

This simple relationship was beginning to unravel. Just as the shift to a mass-manufacturing economy changed virtually every aspect of the economy, so it dramatically affected healthcare. The sheer energy of the economy unleashed resources to treat disease on a massive scale, and the emphasis gradually shifted to research. We saw the rise of large pharmaceutical companies, whose focus and attention was on the eradication of diseases that crippled social and economic progress (and where money could be made). After World War II, the government itself accelerated the trend by granting progressively more funding to medical research. For example, The National Institute for Health started funding research at a low level in the late 1920s. The government also began providing more funding for medical education and training through Medicare. About the same time, the focus shifted from not just healing the patient, but also to eliminating disease.

With this strong emphasis on research and the powerful influx of funding that went with it, the inevitable effect was to create a business sector in its own right, driven, like every other sector, by profit and loss. The scope of research and the costs associated with it required a much more sophisticated financial infrastructure to support the increasing costs incurred by bringing to the patient a growing number of services, new and better medications, and new and more sophisticated technologies. And as the healthcare sector grew, so also the medical insurance sector blossomed. Healthcare was now a serious business.

From Two to Three

Healthcare was indeed a business, but it was becoming a highly regulated one. As the costs of healthcare grew, in terms of both direct costs and the costs of insurance premiums, Western governments stepped in to provide a social safety net, and with their intervention, the door was now open to the separation of delivery and payment. Instead of two at the table, there were now three.

It actually started during World War II. At one point, the government put a cap on the salaries companies could offer, but because companies couldn't compete on compensation, the government allowed them to compete on benefits—which of course focused around healthcare coverage. The separation of healthcare delivery and payment was set in motion.

This separation got a huge boost in the 1960s with the introduction of Medicare. This was a sea change. Insurers now became a potent force in healthcare, and their presence severed any existing financial relationship between the provider and the patient. Before the advent of the third party payer, the discussion between the physician and the patient had always included a discussion about the cost of the treatment, and that discussion often determined the choice of treatment.

With the insertion of third-party payers, the discussion on the cost of treatment disappeared. The governor went off the system. Doctors were still, of course, meeting the needs of their patients, but as a profession, the focus shifted to medical advances, and not to the most efficient and cost-effective ways of delivering healthcare.

These medical advances did indeed save lives, if the patient could afford or access them. But this new focus on medical advances also led to a delivery system that relentlessly developed diagnostics and therapeutics offering hope to patients who found that, with enough pressure, insurance companies and governments were willing to pay. Cost-benefit discussions disappeared, with serious repercussions:

- Little research into technology assessment
- Delayed evaluation and implementation of evidenced-based medical decision making
- Almost no assessments of outcomes, safety, and service
- And worst of all, a failure to link third-party insurance payments to actual patient-specific outcomes, safety, and service.

The Escalation Cycle

The net effect was an escalation cycle. The separation of payment and delivery, of provider and patient, gave providers a newfound freedom to offer services regardless of their cost, since the cost was no longer part of the discussion with the patient. And the ancillary impact was substantial. It soon became evident that these new services were an additional source of revenue, both for the manufacturers and the providers, and the providers soon began to increase the number of services and new approaches they offered.

They also began to advertise their specialties directly to the patient, frequently disguised as information for the public—because the patient wasn't paying for them. For their part, the patients wanted these services, and when the payer didn't cover the service or treatment, they demanded the payer cover them, which in turn escalated the costs and put pressure on the payers to contain those rising costs (as illustrated in the diagram on the next page).

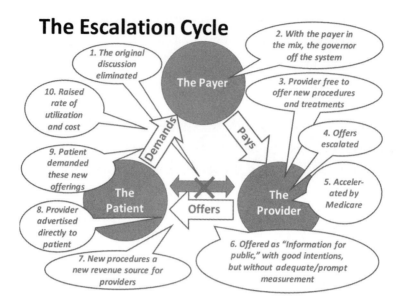

The Escalation Cycle

1. The original discussion eliminated

2. With the payer in the mix, the governor off the system

3. Provider free to offer new procedures and treatments

4. Offers escalated

5. Accelerated by Medicare

6. Offered as "Information for public," with good intentions, but without adequate/prompt measurement

7. New procedures a new revenue source for providers

8. Provider advertised directly to patient

9. Patient demanded these new offerings

10. Raised rate of utilization and cost

The Payer

The Patient

The Provider

Demands

Pays

Offers

In the 1990s, HMOs started to push back, and their pushback came at the interface between the payer and the patient (the upper-left arrow in the diagram above). But as they pushed back, they were met with a backlash from both patients and providers. Aggravating all of this was the federal government's approach to controlling "costs" by setting prices. As the government reduced or slowed the rate of growth for the amount it would pay for each service and procedure, the delivery system compensated by increasing the number of the services and procedures done for patients.

Two features of this escalation are worth highlighting:

1. Healthcare has been totally politicized. Given the universal interest in healthcare and the nature of regulated industries, such politicization was inevitable. Whether good or bad, it is a fact of life, and a lasting solution will require a political dimension as well as an execution dimension.

2. Healthcare coverage has come to be seen as a right, perhaps justifiably so. It wasn't always a given: even as recently as the seventies, healthcare coverage was viewed as an option, and most opted not to take it. Healthcare coverage at that time was like dental insurance today: a

personal option, useful if you needed major dental procedures, okay if you could afford it, and certainly not a right.

Whatever the solutions for healthcare, they will have to factor in these two realities.

Such, then, has been the escalation cycle. In effect, as a payer who was different from the consumer was inserted into the mix, as we said earlier, the governor came off the system.[2] And in coming off the system, the cycle has accelerated, and we are out of control.

But we shouldn't be surprised. The system has given an entirely rational response to the incentives it has created—a system based on fee for service, with managed price controls and managed payment levels, based on a scale of value attached to each delivery function (what the healthcare industry calls "relative value units" or RVUs), high for specialists and low for primary and general care—all of which has led to a "rational" business response to a delivery system that drives each healthcare sector to maximize its own interests. The result is huge waste in healthcare delivery, with a lot of high-cost specialists.

But we are getting ahead of ourselves. In the next chapter, we'll outline exactly what problems this dysfunctional system has created. And knowing how we got here, you won't be surprised by just how serious they are.

---

2 For a view of the evolution of the insurance side of healthcare, see the following site: http://eh.net/encyclopedia/health-insurance-in-the-united-states/

Chapter 3

The Depth of the Problem
The Impact of Losing Sight of the Patient

The history of the healthcare industry helps us understand the sheer depth of the problem. It should also show us how over the years, as the problem fermented and expanded, we lost even greater sight of the patient. Like a ship traveling away from the harbor, the light of reference got progressively dimmer, until it was completely extinguished and we couldn't locate the point of origin.

Great leaders solve big problems. More accurately, they create the environments where big problems can be solved. In fact one of the critical measures of leadership is its ability to bring a lasting solution to a persistent and ever-growing problem. The more significant the problem, the stronger the call for great leadership to facilitate its solution.

Healthcare delivery is such a problem. The issues within healthcare began as a small snowball at the top of the mountain, but it is now traveling downhill, with great momentum and mass, and at times seems completely unstoppable. Whoever stops this avalanche will earn the undying gratitude of every present and future patient that goes through its system, which is every one of us. Such leaders may not be publicly visible, but those who know them will justly elevate their leadership to greatness.

So with this in mind, how do we describe the problem in healthcare that our fearless leaders need to solve?

Consider the following story as a metaphor for healthcare. Many years ago, the residents of a village in Canada built their community next to a river. At a certain point, they noticed a growing number of drowning deaths due to the river's swift current. So, they implemented elaborate measures to save the townspeople. Talk to them today, and they'll proudly speak about the hospital by the edge of the water, the rescue boats at the ready, and the many dedicated lifeguards willing to risk their lives. So preoccupied were these heroic villagers with rescue and treatment that they never thought to look upstream to find out what caused people to fall into the river. A better solution would have been to prevent people from falling into the river in the first place.[3]

The same is true in healthcare. We often look at the wrong entry point to diagnose the problem. To solve it well, you have to frame it well. How you frame a problem matters: it determines its solution, and we should work to frame it in terms of primary causes rather than secondary ones. It is all too easy and all too frequent to settle on a secondary cause in the mistaken belief that you are dealing with a primary cause—and thus ignore the real cause, just like the small village that focused on saving the people who fell in the water instead of preventing them from falling in the first place. It's a lot easier to build a fence than to build a hospital. We frequently and unwittingly address symptoms under the mistaken assumption that we are addressing the disease.

So what are these problems? And what is the driving problem?

If a magic genie were to give us one wish to cure healthcare—and only one—we know what it would be: a common purpose and vision, shared by all, replacing the multitude of competing purposes and visions that proliferate healthcare. That may not sound like something particularly significant, but don't be fooled—it is. If healthcare delivery as a whole embraced a common purpose and a common vision, healthcare delivery would be transformed.

---

3   Source: Sustainability Primer, United States Edition. By the Natural Step Canada (https://www.iusb.edu/csfuture/docs/tnsprimer). Adapted from Steingraber, S. (1997). Living Downstream: an Ecologist Looks at Cancer and the Environment. Addison Wesley.

Where All the Problems Begin ...

```
┌─────────────────────────────┐
│ 1  Lack of Common Purpose   │        A
│    Lack of Common Vision    │   Leadership
└─────────────────────────────┘      Issue!
              ↓
      ┌────────────────────┐
      │ Multiple, Competing │
      │ Purposes and Visions│
      └────────────────────┘
              ↓
   ┌───────────────────────────────┐
   │ 2 Fractured and Limited Interface │
   │   Among the Main Domains of Healthcare │
   └───────────────────────────────┘
        ↓                    ↓
┌──────────────┐      ┌──────────────┐
│ An Inconsistent, │   │ A Dysfunctional │
│ Low-Value, Poorly│   │ Payment        │
│ 3 Functioning System│ │ System    4    │
└──────────────┘      └──────────────┘
        ↓                    ↓
┌──────────────┐      ┌──────────────┐
│ 5 A Misplaced Focus│ │ Increasingly   │
│   on Acute Care  │   │ Escalating Costs 6│
└──────────────┘      └──────────────┘
```

Where stakeholders compete to meet their own interests—and not those of the patient!

Incentivizing the wrong things!

A common purpose and vision are the starting point, and their absence triggers everything else that plagues healthcare (as illustrated in the diagram above). If we can develop a common purpose and a common vision, and eliminate or sublimate the multiple, competing purposes and visions in the healthcare industry, every other problem that plagues healthcare delivery would be resolved.

So, in addition to the absence of a common purpose and a common vision, what are the key issues in healthcare? Here the critical problems, as we see them, captured in the diagram above:

1. *The absence of a common purpose and vision—and the proliferation of competing purposes and visions*
2. *The fractured and limited interface between healthcare delivery and the other domains of healthcare*
3. *An inconsistent, low-value, poorly functioning system*
4. *A dysfunctional payment system*
5. *The focus of healthcare delivery on acute care*
6. *The excessive and escalating cost of healthcare.*

Let's unpack each one in turn.

1. The Absence of a Common Purpose and Vision—and the Proliferation of Competing Purposes and Visions

First and foremost, healthcare delivery needs a purpose and a vision that put the patient firmly at the center of healthcare delivery.

In the absence of such a purpose and vision, the system has degenerated into the self-centered pursuit of the personal priorities of all the other stakeholders. In the current system, stakeholders work individually to *maximize* their own personal interests rather than work collaboratively to *optimize* the functioning of the system for the benefit of patients.

But the good news is that it can be changed. The power of a clear purpose and a strong vision, focused on the interests of the patient, will allow the healthcare delivery system to self-organize with the patient in the center.

The Importance of Purpose and Vision—and the Pain of their Absence

Why are purpose and vision so important? Imagine a Roman chariot behind a set of strong, powerful, and intimidating Arabian mares, all at full gallop. In the chariot is not just one charioteer, but several, and they are fighting each other for the control of the chariot. And as that chariot lurches and races out of control, it destroys wheat fields, gardens, walls, and people … pretty much anything in its path.

The chariot leaves behind a wake of destruction. The question is who is actually driving the destruction? While it is the mass and friction from the horses and the chariot that cause the physical damage, they are just an extension of the drivers. The drivers, and their competing interests, are to blame. No one in their right mind would blame the horses or the man who built the chariot. The horses are the secondary causes; they are propelled by a primary cause.

In healthcare, the chariot is not driven by people, but by a state of mind. That state of mind is the total absence of a common purpose and a common vision—and in their absence, a proliferation of competing purposes and visions surface. There is no harmony, no synchronicity. Healthcare in America is an internecine warzone, a battlefield of competing interests.

Purpose and vision *do* matter. In fact they are so important that we later devote a whole chapter to each one. The difference in outcomes between these two contrasting visions of healthcare—one with the patient at the center and the other with everyone else at the center—is profound. This isn't just an academic exercise: it's an intensely personal matter, because sooner or later, we all become patients and the system we are trying to fix is the very one in which we will find ourselves. Patients are not an abstract entity: they are our family, our friends, our colleagues—in fact each of us. The litmus test we should all be applying is this: *What kind of care would we want for ourselves and for our family?*

We can draw a lesson from systems thinking. If systems thinking sounds like a difficult and abstract concept, its essence is captured in a simple diagram called the SIPOC model (see below), popularized in the 1990s by Six Sigma (a tool for analyzing and redesigning virtually any kind of work process). The SIPOC model is an acronym that contains five elements: *Supplier, Input, Process, Output,* and *Customer.*

SIPOC Model
The Big Picture

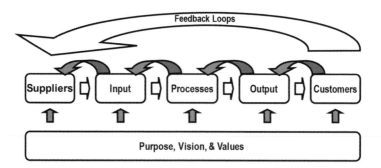

Logic would suggest that we start from the left and work our way to the right. In reality, we need to start from the right and work to the left. Our first question is this: what does the customer want? If we know what the customer wants, we can determine the outputs the customer is looking for.

Once we identify the desired outputs, we can then determine the processes we need in order to provide that output.

And once we have identified the processes we need to produce that output, we can identify the inputs we need to effectively perform the processes that will produce the desired output.

And when we have defined the inputs, we can determine who will supply those inputs.

Notice that there is a constant feedback loop—each stage providing feedback to the previous stage, and each stage grounded in the mission, vision, and values.

Does the Healthcare Industry Apply this Model?

In short, it does not. In the healthcare industry, we have put the wrong person in the customer box. We have put a whole slew of people in that box other than the customer. These include employers, employees, providers, insurers, pharmaceutical companies, imaging and biotech companies, innovators and inventors, politicians, lawyers, policy makers and consultants. The system produces outputs that are designed to satisfy and even maximize the self-interest of just about everyone … except the individual that needs it the most.

2. The Fractured and Limited Interface between Healthcare Delivery and the Other Domains of Healthcare

The healthcare system is composed of five distinct domains:

1. The knowledge domain
2. The payer domain
3. The medical legal domain
4. The regulatory domain
5. The healthcare delivery domain

In reality, the healthcare system is in fact a collection of systems, with each domain acting as a system in its own right. Collectively, they act together as a system of systems.

The knowledge domain reflects what we know and what we are discovering about medicine. Medical research continues to expand its frontiers, and as it does, some of its discoveries find their way into the healthcare delivery domain. The payer domain—equally divorced from the healthcare delivery domain—is reluctant to acknowledge these advances (because of their initial costs) and is therefore unwilling to reimburse them until forced to do so. The legal domain is smaller, but significant, and the pervasive reality of lawsuits has created an adversarial interface between the legal community and the healthcare delivery community. All these domains are directly and powerfully shaped by the fourth domain—the regulatory domain.

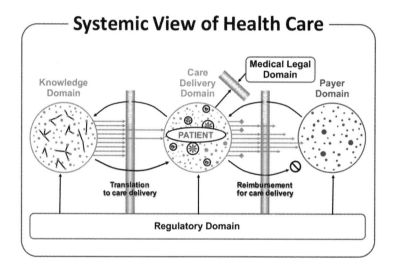

The problem is this: in our current system, as illustrated in the diagram above, the interface structures between these domains severely limit and handicap their communication and interaction.

Reconfiguring this interface is the focus of later chapters. Whatever that reconfiguration looks like, it will inevitably assign a critical role to the providers of healthcare. Why? Because they alone sit at the nexus of all the domains—which is where the patient is, or should be, at the center.

3. An Inconsistent, Low-Value, Poorly Functioning System

It is tempting to think of US healthcare as a monolithic, uniform delivery system—one that is monolithically and uniformly bad. Politicians and pundits make sweeping comparisons with Canada, Great Britain, Germany, and Japan, as if the entire US healthcare system were a homogeneous system with no differences between Miami and Wisconsin.

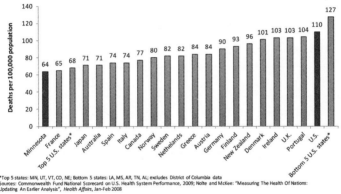

The Same U.S. Health System: Some of the Best and Worst Mortality Outcomes in the World

Mortality related to healthcare: deaths before age 75 that are potentially preventable with timely and appropriate medical care
(International data 2002-2003, State data 2004-2005)

*Top 5 states: MN, UT, VT, CO, NE; Bottom 5 states: LA, MS, AR, TN, AL; excludes District of Columbia data
Sources: Commonwealth Fund National Scorecard on U.S. Health System Performance, 2009; Nolte and McKee: "Measuring The Health Of Nations: Updating An Earlier Analysis", *Health Affairs*, Jan-Feb 2008

The reality is otherwise. The quality of healthcare service is hugely variable and uneven. The differences are huge, and not just between Miami and Wisconsin. The top five states in the US rank consistently in the top three national comparisons, and the bottom five limp along with the bottom-ranked global healthcare systems.

Unfortunately, the top five aren't good enough to keep the US as a whole from crawling along at the bottom of the charts, and as an aggregate, the US does not fare well. These extraordinary differences are in themselves evidence of a poorly functioning system. The system itself is incapable of sharing best practices. Unfortunately, it is very adept at propagating its worst practices.

This variable and uneven service is evident in multiple areas, and even in places you would least expect it. For example, you would expect teaching hospitals across the country to deliver pretty consistent outcomes. Because of their access to the latest technology, you would expect them to perform better than other hospitals. But the differences among these hospitals are significant.

In the table below, the mortality ratio is a function of expected deaths divided by actual deaths. So "1" is even: there were no unexpected deaths, and none of the deaths that were expected were prevented. Greater than 1 is good: it tells us that the institution did an excellent job of reducing the number of actual deaths—less than the expected number. Less than 1 is bad— the institution had more deaths than it expected, and by inference, they could potentially have been prevented.

COTH Hospitals4	Mortality Ratio >1 = Better Than Expected
Best Hospital in Category	2.06
Worst Hospital in Category	0.65
Teaching Hospital Average	**1.02**

The difference between the best and the worst is more than threefold for hospitals that would have the highest likelihood of even and uniform service. Similarly, the variability in efficiency and safety in the USA is significant.

Satisfaction with inpatient services is also highly variable. One national survey measured the satisfaction level of patients (across multiple medical conditions) within 48 hours to six weeks of their discharge. At the best-ranked hospitals, 83 percent reported satisfaction, but for patients discharged from hospitals in the bottom five percent, it was only 52 percent.

In all this, it should be obvious that higher spending does not equate to better healthcare outcomes. Some of the most expensive delivery systems are the

---

4   COTH = Council of Teaching Hospitals and Health Systems; n = 269 COTH member facilities; excludes COTH member VA and Children's hospitals; excludes facilities with <50 actual deaths in 2009 Source: https://www.aamc.org/members/coth/; MedPar 2009

least effective. Some of the least expensive are the most effective. This ambiguity and unpredictability is just one example of how poorly the healthcare system functions. It is like playing pin the tail on the donkey while being double blindfolded. Past performance does not predict future results and the empirical or quantifiable data doesn't help us either. We are blindly looking for a solution.

4. A Dysfunctional Payment System

At the heart of US healthcare is a payment system based on fee per service. It is a system inherently and unavoidably designed to drive and incentivize high cost, not great value or customer care.

In our current system, a doctor is paid for performing a procedure or service. It doesn't matter whether the procedure or service works; the doctor is paid anyway. A botched procedure resulting in complications or even death is compensated at the same rate as a successful outcome. Payment is tied to process (a procedure is part of the process) and not to solutions. As we saw from the SIPOC model, when you focus on the processes and not on the outcomes, you end up with unintended consequences (or perhaps intended consequences)— but most importantly, we don't see the outcomes the patient needs or wants. Payments are at their highest when the patient is sick; they are at their lowest when we focus on keeping the patient well.

The current system operates on the following formula:

Total Healthcare Spending = Cost or Price ÷ Unit of Service × Use Rate

Spending reflects the actual revenues for the services rendered. The total posted revenues for all the procedures a hospital offers may come to a total of, say, $3.5 billion. But they know that they can't charge their full fees, and their actual revenues may be closer to $2.1 billion. Why is that? Because the payers won't pay the full rate and they negotiate or dictate a better rate.

Take colonoscopy procedures, using artificial price estimates, as an example. A hospital may set its price at $1,000, but they also know that $1,000 is not what they are going to get paid. Private payers (insurance companies, associations, large employers) will negotiate by starting at $550 and the payer and the provider may settle on a maximum of $600 that the payer is willing to reimburse for a colonoscopy. In the case of the Federal Government, there is no negotiation—they just set the fee, and they might set it as low as $250.

So this puts the hospital in a bind. The hospital leaders know that they have to generate a certain amount of revenues to cover their fixed costs and stay in business. So if the payment is below the total cost of a procedure, performing more procedures is one way to cover these fixed costs. Too often the delivery system has chosen this solution. In the case of the colonoscopy, the provider will tell the patient they need to have a colonoscopy every three years—not five, or even ten. The result? Total cost per patient goes up and so does the amount of times a patient has to experience the unpleasantness (and nominal risk) of a colonoscopy.

Multiply this over the broad spectrum of healthcare, and it should be no surprise that healthcare spending has been escalating on a per-patient basis, as well as on a total-population basis.

5. The Focus of Healthcare Delivery on Acute Care

In the past, the hospital was viewed as the center of the healthcare universe. And in the minds of many, it remains so. However, hospitals exist to solve medical problems, not to prevent them. They are designed for acute care. They need acute care to survive. So it's not surprising that the focus of the healthcare system has been on sick care. Little attention is paid to the health of the general population or to those who are prone to chronic illnesses but haven't yet shown evidence of the disease.

Just how much the current healthcare system revolves around acute care (and how much providers depend on it for their livelihood) becomes clear when we think in terms of four main forms of prevention:

- ***Primary prevention***, which is the first line of prevention, focuses on the general population with the goal of avoiding the occurrence of disease. Educational health promotion programs are examples of primary prevention efforts.

- ***Secondary prevention*** includes educational as well as clinical practice efforts, along with tools to diagnose and treat existing diseases in their early stages. The goal is to prevent the disease from progressing to significant morbidity for the patient.
- ***Tertiary prevention*** targets those in more advanced stages of a disease and who now have more severe symptoms and complications from the disease. The goal of tertiary prevention is to reduce these negative impacts by reducing symptoms and eliminating complications, and thereby restoring and maintaining some measure of functionality and health for the patient.
- ***Quaternary prevention*** refers to the methods used to mitigate or eliminate unnecessary and excessive medical care (whether in terms of diagnostic testing, procedures, interventions, or medication), as well as those methods used to eliminate the side effects and complications from appropriate medications and procedures.

These four approaches to prevention are directly applied to specific segments of the population, and in the diagram below, you will see how people in a given

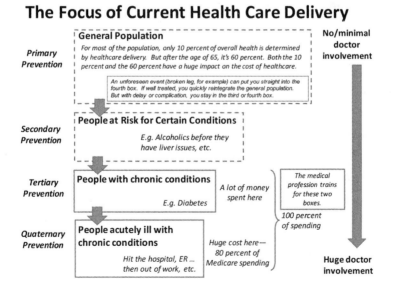

The Focus of Current Health Care Delivery

Primary Prevention

General Population
For most of the population, only 10 percent of overall health is determined by healthcare delivery. But after the age of 65, it's 60 percent. Both the 10 percent and the 60 percent have a huge impact on the cost of healthcare.

An unforeseen event (broken leg, for example) can put you straight into the fourth box. If well treated, you quickly reintegrate the general population. But with delay or complication, you stay in the third or fourth box.

No/minimal doctor involvement

Secondary Prevention

People at Risk for Certain Conditions
E.g. Alcoholics before they have liver issues, etc.

Tertiary Prevention

People with chronic conditions
E.g. Diabetes

A lot of money spent here

The medical profession trains for these two boxes.

100 percent of spending

Quaternary Prevention

People acutely ill with chronic conditions
Hit the hospital, ER ... then out of work, etc.

Huge cost here— 80 percent of Medicare spending

Huge doctor involvement

population might fit into these categories at various times in their lives. The diagram shows how people in an entire population encounter the healthcare delivery system (the lower two boxes) and how people would benefit from broader societal actions to improve health (reflected in the upper two boxes). These four segments are addressed in more detail below.

<u>The General Population</u>

- The general population (the largest box at the top of the diagram) is for the most part functionally healthy. It operates outside of the healthcare system until an accident or an illness puts them into it.

- We call this Primary Prevention: it is at this level that efforts at primary prevention can be most effective, including, for example, promoting education and regulations to control use and abuse of tobacco, alcohol, and drugs, improving health education, and introducing exercise back into schools. Primary prevention requires significant investment, with little hope of return in the short term, but with the hope of possible substantial returns in the long term.

<u>The At-Risk Population</u>

- Of the general population, a portion is at risk for chronic conditions (the second box down). They may not have a particular condition yet, but they are susceptible to it. Alcoholics, for example, may not have liver issues, but they will inevitably develop them. It's difficult to put an overall percentage on this group, because it covers multiple conditions.

- We call this Secondary Prevention: in the current healthcare system, virtually no money is spent on this box, but were it to be spent, the investments would be focused on identifying those at high risk for chronic conditions and preventing the condition from developing.

- Secondary prevention also requires investment of money in the short term with the clear expectation of reduced or delayed expenditure in the longer term. The current system is neither geared to support or to even to afford the interventions encompassed by the first two forms of prevention.

The Population with Chronic Conditions

- Some of those who are at risk for chronic conditions inevitably develop those conditions, and they then fall into the next category—the third box down in the diagram. The list of such conditions is lengthy, and it includes asthma, high blood pressure, cardiovascular conditions, cancer, obesity, chronic obstructive lung disease, HIV, Hepatitis C, degenerative brain diseases, and arthritis. Someone who is obese without diabetes is in the second box (at risk), but when that person develops diabetes, as they inevitably do, they fall into this box. In our current healthcare system, it is at this level that the money starts flowing.

- We call this Tertiary Prevention: at this level, efforts at tertiary prevention have a high likelihood of near-term savings. Direct healthcare savings accrue through reductions in hospital admissions, reductions in emergency visits, and reductions in visits to doctors' offices. While these initiatives may not cure the chronic conditions, more people will live active and productive lives in spite of their medical conditions. More people will enjoy their free time and miss fewer days of work or school.

The Population Acutely Ill with Chronic Conditions

- Those with the chronic conditions (those in the third box down) invariably at some point become acutely ill patients—and they fall into the fourth box at the bottom. Also falling into this last box are people in good health who have an accident or develop an acute medical or surgical condition unrelated to preexisting chronic conditions. In either case, they are frequently seen in medical clinics or emergency rooms and admitted to hospitals.

- At this point, the money is flowing in earnest. It is estimated, for example, that up to 80 percent of Medicare spending is spent in this box. And the total cost is much more than the money that flows in and out of the hospital—these events trigger significant additional intangible costs from lost work and lost productivity, not to mention the social costs (family tensions or loss of time in school, for example), with inevitable negative economic implications.

- We call this Quaternary Prevention: it is in this box that prevention has the potential for great savings, primarily by eliminating waste. Waste comes in two forms:
  - ○ Waste from inefficient delivery—from mistakes and inattentiveness, with unintended complications and infections.
  - ○ Waste from poor choices, however well they are done—procedures done well and with high quality, but totally unnecessary. An unnecessary procedure is still a waste, however well and efficiently it is executed.

Progression through the four boxes is not necessarily sequential. For example, people in the first box (the general population) can land suddenly in the fourth box. Examples like a broken leg, gall bladder, appendicitis, and other acute medical emergencies can take them there very quickly and suddenly. They go in and then come out if they are well treated. But if they are not (if they catch infections, or if procedures for whatever reason don't work), they may end up stuck in the third and fourth.

Serving Our Community? (Denis)

One Sunday, my grandson developed an acute medical problem. The condition could have been handled with a pediatric clinic visit, but the pediatric phone triage nurse could offer the only option we hear far too often: "Go to the ER." When we arrived at the hospital, we found a large section under renovation and expansion, with an imposing sign that read: "Excuse this mess—we are expanding to serve our community better!" However well intentioned, this sign was a perfect illustration of our healthcare problem. Increasing the size of a hospital is not the best way to serve the community. Finding ways to keep people out of the hospital would be of far greater service to its community.

The current system rewards the third and fourth boxes—the two that reside at the bottom. It actually does more than reward those two boxes—by the incentives it creates it *drives* people into those two boxes. From a hospital's viewpoint, sicker people equates to better business. But from a patient's perspective, the goal should be to push as many people out of the fourth box and into the third, and as many as possible out of the third box and into the second, and eventually, as many as possible out of the second box and into the first. We need to reverse the incentives—away from a focus on acute care and towards a destination of healthier lives.

6. The Excessive and Escalating Cost of Healthcare

Healthcare in America is expensive; in fact, it is more expensive than anywhere else on the planet. Per capita, it has a higher cost than any other country. In fact, at just under $8,000 per capita, it is almost double Canada's per capita cost, pretty much double France's per capita cost, and more than double the per capita cost in the UK.[5]

What drives the costs?

- *The lack of focus on the patient.* If you focus on the processes without regard to the outcomes, you inevitably create waste and duplication, which raises costs.
- *The excessive focus on acute care.* Sadly, costs will escalate if the only option for an adult or a child is an emergency room without recourse to primary care. In many cities and rural areas, even during regular weekday working hours (8:00 a.m. to 5:00 p.m.), the only option is an emergency room visit.
- *The legal costs.* Lawyers drive up medical costs. One 2005 survey indicated that almost all physicians (93 percent) practice defensive medicine (ordering tests or procedures to avoid possible future malpractice lawsuits), more than half (59 percent) admitted to ordering more tests than necessary, just over half (52 percent) said they referred patients to

5   OECD Health Data figures 2011, for the year 2009.

other doctors in unnecessary circumstances, and one third (33 percent) said they often prescribed more medications than medically necessary.[6] In a 2006 study, PriceWaterhouseCoopers put the combined cost of defensive medicine and the associated legal costs at somewhere between $50 billion and $200 billion. We aren't talking about chump change.

But the real issue in the legal environment is not the money. The real cost—and this cost is much greater than the $50-200 billion cited above—is the cost that comes from muzzling problem-solving measures. From a systems perspective, the legal environment is a demilitarized zone where no one treads for fear of coming under fire. The result is an absolute lack of transparency that makes it that much harder to avoid making the same mistake that generated the lawsuit in the first place. We need to run healthcare investigations in the same way that some federal agencies run theirs—such as the Federal Aviation Administration, the National Transportation Safety Board, and the Institute of Nuclear Power Operations. Accidents, near misses, and mistakes are openly and fully investigated, and the findings and recommendations are promulgated throughout their respective industries.

- *The advances in technology.* The US has the greatest access to the latest technology. Compared to Canada, France, and the UK, for instance, the US has three to five times as many MRI machines.

U.S. Much Higher Access to Expensive Medical Technology

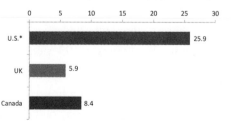

MRI machines per million population (2010)

U.S.* 25.9
UK 5.9
Canada 8.4

*US data is 2007
Source: OECD Health Data, 2011

- ***The inefficiencies in delivery.*** Inefficiencies create medical errors, and these raise the cost of and spending for healthcare. A 1999 report by the Institute of Medicine estimated that avoidable medical errors contributed to annual deaths between 44,000 and 98,000 in the US. A 2010 report by the Department of Health and Human Services indicated that little has changed, and put the additional Medicare cost of "adverse events" in 2008 at $4.4 billion. The Denver Health Practice of Milliman (one of the world's largest actuarial and consulting firms) estimated that for the same year (2008), medical errors cost the US approximately $17.1 billion.

These factors represent a huge amount of waste in healthcare. In fact the Institute of Medicine (now called the National Academy of Medicine)[7] has compiled the annual waste in healthcare:

Area	*Annual Cost*
Unnecessary Care	$210 billion
Inefficient Care	$130 billion
Excess Administrative Costs	$190 billion
Inflated Prices	$105 billion
Prevention	$55 billion
Fraud	$75 billion

This comes to an estimated total of $765 billion in 2009. Notice that the first two—a little less than half of the total—reflect what doctors, nurses, pharmacists, and hospital administrators can actually control! These two are clearly in the domain of the providers, but they are not the only ones: even inflated prices and prevention are partially in their hands, and so, some would argue, is fraud.

Assuming that the IOM numbers are correct, we can make the following observations:

---

7   For more information, see http://resources.iom.edu/widgets/vsrt/healthcare-waste.html

- The approach of dealing with global budget and price controls will only address "Inflated Prices" ($105 billion).
- Paying for value will address unnecessary and inefficient care, prevention, and fraud (a total of $470 billion).
- Administrative simplification will help with the remaining $190 billion.

Based on the above estimates of waste, The Institute of Medicine has also identified potential savings per year, obtainable over the next ten years with the actions listed in the table below.[8]

Action	Savings
Streamline administrative costs	$181 billion
Improve hospital efficiency	$80 billion
Decrease costs for each episode of care	$53 billion
Avoid preventable admissions	$48 billion
Improve targeted costly services	$20 billion
Prevent avoidable readmissions	$20 billion
Prevent medical errors	$12 billion
Increase highly-informed, shared decision-making with the patient	$9 billion

With a total of $423 billion, this represents about 18 percent of the $2.5 trillion spent in the year of the study.[9] (The estimate for 2015 was over $3 trillion spent on healthcare.) If we then add the IOM estimate of $30 billion a year in malpractice reform, and another $10 billion a year in fraud and abuse prevention, within ten years, we come to an impressive $463 billion a year in total savings.[10]

---

8   Numbers in the table presented in *The Healthcare Imperative: Lowering Costs and Improving Outcomes,* Workshop Series Summary, delivered by the Institute of Medicine's Roundtable on Value &Science-Driven Healthcare. Pierre L. Yong, Robert S. Saunders, and Leigh Anne Olson, Editors, Institute of Medicine of the National Academies. The National Academies Press, released February 24, 2011.

9   See also link on the IOM website http://resources.iom.edu/widgets/vsrt/healthcare-waste.html

10   For another excellent analysis of the cost of waste, see *Eliminating Waste in US Healthcare*, by Donald M. Berwick, MD, MPP and Andrew D. Hackbarth, MPhil, JAMA April 11, 2012, Vol. 307, No. 14

The system has created incentives that reward duplication and inefficiency. Instead of reining in costs, the system supports and even drives their escalation. We would be hard pressed to find an economist to support the kind of price controls we see in healthcare.

And it isn't just the providers who have the incentives to spend more—it's also the patients. When someone else is paying the bill (or most of it), there is little reason to control personal spending.

Back to Leadership

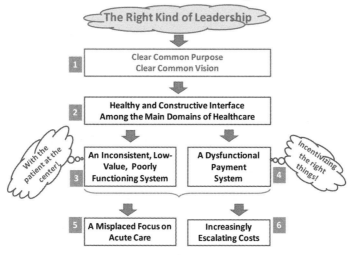

However bleak this may sound, it is far from hopeless. Solutions are available. Remember, great leaders solve big problems. When it comes to leadership, as Sam Walton (the founder of Wal-Mart) once said, "High expectations are the key to everything." We will see a turnaround if we have enough of the right kind of leaders exercising the right kind of leadership in the right places. We just have to expect and even demand more. Just as the problems in healthcare delivery begin with the absence of purpose and vision, so the solutions begin with the presence of leaders collaborating around a common purpose and a common vision for healthcare delivery.

Parts II and III focus on and clarify the exact type of leadership we need to pursue. But before we get there, we have one more question to address: why is leadership so difficult? We need to paint a realistic picture of the leadership challenge we face, because understanding the challenge makes it that much easier to overcome it.

That is the subject of the next chapter.

Chapter 4

Why Is Leadership So Difficult?

I n the previous chapter, we discussed the real-life impact of healthcare's impaired vision—losing sight of the patient. With a basic understanding of that impairment, it should be clear why leadership is so important. But acknowledging its importance doesn't make it any easier to exercise … and if the challenge of leadership sounds daunting, it's no doubt because it actually is. Not only is great leadership critically important, it is also extraordinarily difficult. The exciting news is that there is a solution to inject fundamental leadership into healthcare, and the better we grasp the scope of the challenge, the better the solution we can bring to the table. To this end, we need to probe the depths of the challenge we face. Some of these challenges are universal and present in every sphere of human endeavor, and some are very specific to healthcare, which we address later in the chapter.

The Universal Challenges of Leadership

Leadership is difficult because it is complex. It has become increasingly so, particularly over the last forty years. We lead in an increasingly complex world, a fact our greatest leaders recognize. The military has a term for it: they call this a "VUCA" world—their acronym for "volatile, uncertain, complex, and ambiguous." That is indeed the kind of world in which we lead.

The early 1980s saw us experience a shift that thrust us decisively into a global economy driven by information technology. That shift had a huge impact on leadership because it changed the conditions in which leaders operate[11]. It changed these conditions in at least five ways that still impact us all today:

- *The expectations placed on leaders have never been as high.* The higher expectations require that leaders have to learn quicker, perform sooner, and understand that tolerance for failure is lower. The honeymoon is shorter, and the learning curve is steeper.
- *The scope of responsibility has never been as broad, both geographically and functionally.* As organizations have become flatter, and as middle management roles have been eliminated, the span of control has widened. More people report to fewer leaders.
- *The scrutiny has never been as intense.* After Sarbanes-Oxley, a financial oversight law passed in 2002,[12] no segment of the economy was left untouched, but in a sector as regulated as healthcare, that scrutiny has been particularly intense, driven both by widespread public interest and by intense political debate.
- *The structures of organizations have never been as complex.* The demands for growth mean that at some point organizations can no longer satisfy their constituencies or stakeholders with organic growth, and so they opt for mergers, acquisitions, joint ventures, and partnerships that may bring growth, but that also create extraordinarily complex leadership environments.
- *The pace of technological change and innovation creates a backdrop that can drastically change the competitive landscape* … a huge challenge for every leader, no matter what sector you lead in, but particularly so in

---

11 For an overview of the way the conditions of leadership have changed over the last thirty years, see *Great Leadership: What It Is and What It Takes in a Complex World*, Antony Bell, Chapter 2 "The Source of Our Confusion."

12 The Sarbanes-Oxley Act, passed in 2002 by the U.S. Congress, was designed to protect investors from the possibility of fraudulent accounting. It produced strict reforms designed to improve financial disclosures.

healthcare, where the pace of change in medical technology far outstrips the pace of change in medical delivery.

As the leadership environment has become more complex, proposed leadership solutions have mushroomed—they have come from every conceivable angle of leadership. Over the last thirty years, we have seen a huge proliferation of disciplines directly related to leadership. The result? Leadership has become multi-faceted. Take a look at the list below—every one of these functions and disciplines represents a skill that at some level and in some way is critical to leadership.

- Strategic Thinking
- Competitive Advantage
- Market Analysis
- Corporate Direction and Focus
- Vision Casting
- Marketing Strategies
- Corporate Alignment
- Corporate Culture
- Corporate Life Cycles
- Critical Success Factors
- Communications Strategy
- Corporate Values Clarification
- Merger and Acquisition Integration
- Acquisition Management
- Financial Acumen
- Organizational Design
- Organizational Development
- Systems Thinking
- Business Process Reengineering
- TQM (Total Quality Management)
- Six Sigma

- Balanced Scorecard
- Transactional Leadership
- Operational Efficiency
- Execution
- Team Building
- Partnering
- Personal Leadership Qualities
- Moral Compass
- Self-Awareness
- Emotional Intelligence
- Relational Capacity
- Use of Assessment Instruments
- Succession Planning
- Performance Management
- Talent Selection
- Talent Development
- Leadership Development
- Coaching
- Mentoring
- Motivation
- Situational Leadership
- Delegation
- Empowerment

This is an encompassing list, but it is not complete. New expressions or variations on these disciplines make their way into the market all the time. Very few leaders read, which is unfortunate, because great leaders are readers. But when you look at this list, we understand why—Where do you (as a leader) even begin?

This list also tells us something else. No single leader can master all these elements, and the best leaders build teams that reflect everything their context needs, while discarding what isn't. Great leaders select to their weakness and to the organization's advantage.

||||||||||||||||||||||||||||||||||||||||||||||||||||||||||||||||||||||||||||||||||||||||||||||||||||||||||||||||||||||||||||||||||||||

Where Do You Start? (Antony)

One of my wife's cousins is the CFO of a medium-sized business in Ohio. He once told me that the thing he hates the most is when his boss (the CEO) goes on vacation. Every time he goes on vacation, he takes a book with him—a business book. When he comes back, the whole company shifts in the direction of that book. The next time he goes on vacation, it's a different book ... and the company lurches in the direction of this new book.

The CEO's problem is that he has no framework to shape his leadership. He's not sure where to start, so he picks haphazardly, without understanding the real needs of his company and the real demands on his leadership. He needs a framework.

||||||||||||||||||||||||||||||||||||||||||||||||||||||||||||||||||||||||||||||||||||||||||||||||||||||||||||||||||||||||||||||||||||||

The Challenges Specific to Healthcare

Any attempt at great leadership in healthcare will need to cope with two challenges:

1. The sheer multitude of stakeholders on the one hand
2. The tension between their competing interests on the other

In 1944, Jean-Paul Sartre published an existentialist play called *No Exit*. The play describes how three damned souls are ushered into hell and find themselves locked together in a single room. At first delighted to have avoided the torture instruments they were expecting, they soon figure out that each one is the other's hell. Each one wants from one of the others something that he or she is unwilling or unable to give. One of the three protagonists famously concludes, *L'enfer, c'est les autres* ("Hell is other people").

In Chapter Two, we introduced the five domains in healthcare:

- The Care-Delivery Domain
- The Knowledge Domain
- The Payer Domain
- The Medical-Legal Domain
- The Regulatory Domain.

The relationship between the five may not be quite as destructive and hopeless as those Sartre described, but each one wants from the other something they are unwilling or unable to give.

Yet herein lie both the challenge and the hope. The challenge is this: How do we get a large number of experts in their disparate fields to come together and work collectively and collaboratively in the pursuit of a vision much bigger than themselves, their self-interest, their company, their law practice, their medical practice, and their politics, all for the benefit of people and patients?

The hope is this: There are many stakeholders across these domains, and many more in each of the domains. With enough stakeholders who touch multiple domains working together, we can actually create momentum around such a vision. We can make beautiful music that the vast audience of healthcare will genuinely enjoy and appreciate … which brings us to the useful metaphor of a magnificently functioning orchestra.

Healthcare as an Orchestra

Roger Nierenberg is an orchestra conductor who has used live orchestras as an illustration of organizational behavior.[13]

---

13   See Roger Nierenberg's book *Maestro—Leading by Listening*. The Penguin Group, 2009

When one of us (Denis) was practicing at the Mayo Clinic in Jacksonville, Florida, in the mid-1990s, Roger and the Jacksonville Symphony Orchestra gave a presentation for our senior administration and clinical staff. It was a fascinating experience.

He started by directing our staff to sit in assigned chairs dispersed throughout the orchestra, and then began to conduct the orchestra in a piece of well-known classical music. After a few minutes, he stopped and asked the participants to describe what they heard—next to them and behind them. Those with the brass heard only the brass, and those with the strings heard mostly strings. Wherever our people were sitting, each one best heard the instruments next to them and behind them—and often it was the *only* thing they heard. We can certainly relate to this in healthcare—we tend to hear only the sounds coming from our particular area of focus.

Nierenberg then resumed the music, but instructed the orchestra to play as loudly as possible. After a few minutes, he stopped the orchestra and asked the participants what they heard. It actually made no difference—they still only heard what was around them. When everyone is clamoring loudly for his or her own interests, it makes no difference: others still don't hear and they still don't get heard. And most importantly, for those outside the orchestra— the audience—the music was horrible. Clamoring more loudly for our own particular self-interest doesn't make us heard any better—and the overall healthcare outcome is horrible.

After these two iterations, he asked the orchestra to play slightly out of tune. They started, but they actually couldn't keep it up. After the first few bars, these professional musicians began listening to those around them and making the adjustments to stay in tune with those they could hear—with the net result that before long, the whole orchestra was playing in tune. Roger Nierenberg made a strong point of this: in a culture that places a high value on collaboration (such as an orchestra, where collaborating and listening to each other are deeply ingrained), it's difficult to stay out of tune and discordant for long. Collaborative cultures, organizations and sectors are self-tuning—and self-correcting. There is a powerful lesson here for leaders in healthcare: promote a culture of collaboration, and people will look for ways to collaborate.

After asking the orchestra to play out of tune, he asked them to play at a different tempo—different to the one they were accustomed to and different to the tempo the music called for. They sustained this a little longer, but again not for long. These professionals could not resist self-organizing themselves to work together and to do it right.

Then came the most striking lesson of all. He asked all the participants sitting dispersed in the orchestra to come to the front and stand behind him while he conducted the orchestra in a repetition of the four demonstrations he had just taken them through. The contrast was striking: when we stood behind the conductor, we heard the whole, not just the section we were originally assigned to. And most of all, we had a tremendous sense of how much the orchestra was an entire living organism, with life waving across it … a very different experience from the one sitting dispersed among the orchestra players.

Orchestras and Healthcare

The challenge for leadership in healthcare is to play as an orchestra—to see and hear the whole, not just our own section—to find common ground and common cause.

And the challenge is daunting. But bringing together the five domains of healthcare, and all those within the five domains, to function as an orchestra is absolutely essential for improving outcomes, safety, service, and the general health of people. And it is essential for controlling the costs of care by eliminating waste.

To highlight these ongoing challenges, consider the following:

- As we have seen, the differences in healthcare delivery are huge when the patient is at the center instead of the self-centered priorities of all the other stakeholders. The challenge is getting the orchestra to play the same music.

- Without a clear vision for patient-centered healthcare, leaders in every domain are confused: do they concentrate only on what is best for the patient or do we encourage them to maximize their own sector? Do we sell more products or do we support research to see how well and for whom the products work, even if it means this research might quickly reveal that the products are worthless? Do we concentrate on treating people in hospitals when they are sick, or do we find ways to pay to treat them at home or, better yet, to prevent people from becoming sick?

- Without a clear vision and a clear sense of purpose for healthcare delivery, priorities become confused and misplaced, with the inevitable result that all stakeholders work to maximize their personal interest rather than work collaboratively to optimize the functioning of the system for the benefit of patients.
- The payment system (fee for service) pays when people are sick. Preventing people from becoming ill means losing money, which makes it very difficult for leaders to jeopardize the financial well being of their organizations, and the security of their job, to work for a noble cause that has no national momentum or validation.
- Leading from vision requires leaders to begin thinking in systems and teamwork, and to build operational leaders, giving up the right to be a boss who can just tell people what to do.

Responding to these challenges will require leadership—great leadership. This country needs leaders from all the healthcare domains to develop the vision, strategy, and implementation needed to bring the five different sections of the healthcare orchestra together in one harmonious whole—instead of a cacophonous group of musicians, deaf to the music being played elsewhere on the stage. It is a conundrum. The hardest goal is to get everyone to play harmoniously together, but the only way we will build a platform to fix the problem of healthcare is to synchronize and harmonize our instruments.

To complicate the task, there are a lot of musicians: the sheer number of healthcare stakeholders is daunting, as illustrated in the two tables at the end of the chapter.

In healthcare's current form, these stakeholders operate much like isolated islands, warding off the encroachments of every other island in the healthcare delivery system—much like the diagram below.

The Key Players— with Competing Interests

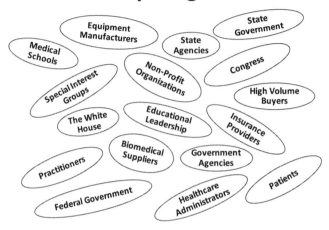

Instead of viewing leadership as a series of disconnected small islands, imagine what it would be like if these five domains did indeed play together as a single orchestra. Instead of a healthcare delivery system populated by independent fiefdoms protecting their territorial gains, it would look something like this:

The Key Players— Working to the Same End

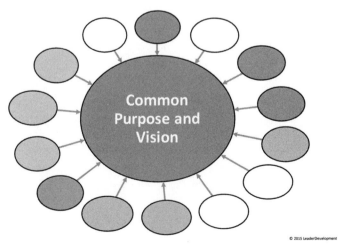

© 2015 LeaderDevelopment Inc.

At this point, all this may sound unrealistic and utopian. No leader could possibly, by sheer force of will or strength of personality, impose the kind of collaboration and harmony such collaboration presupposes.

We agree. The real question is this: who is the conductor that brings it all together and organizes the musicians to play together? For purposes of healthcare, the conductor is not a person. The conductor is a common purpose, a common vision, and a common set of values. If the entire orchestra can be synchronized by a common purpose, a common vision, and a common set of values, it will produce inspiring music.

So what does that purpose look like?
What does that vision look like?
And what are those common values?

That is the subject of Part II.

Current Roles Played by Each Domain

Care Delivery Domain	Knowledge Domain	Payer Domain	Medical Legal Domain	Regulatory Domain
Diagnosis Treatment Rehabilitation Prevention	Medical-related education Clinical training Research Innovation Medical technologies Data Collection Measurement	Reimbursement Patient coverage	Confidential and undiscoverable malpractice procedures Compensation for patients and families State specific policies	Numerous policy and regulations related to the following: Health Medical documentation Billing codes Payments Use of information technology Clinical certification and licenses State specific scope of practice for providers State specific insurance rules

Key Stakeholders in Each Domain

Care-Delivery Domain	Knowledge Domain	Payer Domain	Medical Legal Domain	Regulatory Domain
• Patients • Physicians • Non-physician providers (pharmacists, physician assistants, nurses, social workers, registered dieticians/ nutritionists, community health workers, physical, occupational, speech therapists, public health workers) • Health care administrators • Public health departments • Community health centers • Sub-acute care facilities	• Medical schools • Dental schools • Nursing schools • Physician assistant programs • Physical, occupation, speech therapy programs • Researchers • Universities • Private Foundations • US Public Health Service (AHRQ, ATSDR, CDC, FDA, HRSA, HIS, NIH, SAMHSA) • State Departments of Health • Professional associations • Trade associations	• Commercial insurers • Self-insured employers • Government payers (Medicare/ Medicaid, Veterans Affairs, Tricare, Indian Health Services, Federal Employees Health Benefits, State Children's Health Insurance Program) • Individual/ Consumers/ Patient	• Lawyers • State Government • Justice system	• Congress • The White House • Federal government agencies • State government agencies • Accreditation agencies including professional specialty boards for providers

• Ambulatory surgery centers • Hospitals • Home health agencies • Rehabilitation centers • Skilled nursing facilities • Nursing homes • Hospices • Integrated networks • Diagnostic clinics • Imaging units • Laboratory services • Health information technology • Non-profit/special interest organizations	• Medical equipment manufacturers • Biomedical suppliers • Pharmaceutical companies • Biotechnology companies • Non-profit/special interest organizations			

The acronyms in the table stand for the following: AHRQ: Agency for Healthcare Research & Quality, ATSDR: Agency for Toxic Substance and Disease Registry, CDC: Centers for Disease Control and Prevention, FDA: Food and Drug Administration, HRSA: Health Resources and Services Administration, IHS: Indian Health Service, NIH: National Institutes of Health, SAMHSA: Substance Abuse and Mental Health Services Administration.

PART II

The *Real* Solution in Healthcare: The Transformation Leaders Need to Lead

*The "Why" of healthcare delivery—what exactly
it is trying to accomplish—needs clarification.*

That is a leadership function.

*The "What" of healthcare delivery—what should
it look like in the future—needs clarification.*

That too is a leadership function.

*The "How" of healthcare delivery—how it is organized and how it
builds itself as a learning system—needs clarification and implementation.*

That too is a leadership function.

Leadership matters.

Chapter 5

Why Healthcare and What Is Its Purpose?

W hy?" is a powerful question. Answer that question and you can move mountains. It is in fact the very first question we need to ask, and absolutely where we begin the conversation. Why do we provide healthcare? To what end? It may seem like an obvious question, and maybe even so obvious that we don't need to ask it. But how we answer it determines everything, and if there is one thing that derails individuals, organizations, and industries more than anything else, it's failing to define a clear purpose and sense of direction, or losing sight of it once they have it. That is why we have to address the "Why?"

It's tempting to skip the "why" and go straight to the "what" question. But only when we have answered the "why" question can we then address the "what" question. This includes:

- What do we want healthcare to look like in the future?
- Where do we want healthcare to go?
- What does it look like when we get there?

The reality is that if we haven't defined the purpose for the journey of healthcare, we cannot define its destination.

To complicate matters, there is more than one way to define its purpose. To help us narrow our choices, let's start by clarifying what it isn't. Among the problems we identified in Chapter Three, three in particular stand out:

1. There is no common purpose or vision to treat the patient as the customer.
2. The interface between healthcare delivery and the other domains of healthcare is fractured and limited.
3. The focus of healthcare is on acute care.

Whatever the purpose of healthcare, it should be the antithesis of these problems. The one common thread these problems maintain is their focus on treating illnesses rather than actually working to prevent them. This tells us that there are at least two ways we can answer the "why" question:

1. Healthcare is designed primarily to *treat* illness.
2. Or it is designed primarily to *prevent* illness.

That may seem like an oversimplification, and even an unnecessary polarization. But Chapter Three showed us that the current healthcare system is built around the first—treating illness. It thrives on a sick population. It exists to treat sickness, not to prevent it, and it has no incentive to reduce the size of the sick population. Sadly, it has every incentive to expand it.

Focusing on the Patient, not on Acute Care

However we define the purpose of healthcare, it has to be centered firmly on the patient. It cannot be focused on acute care.

If you were to ask anyone to name the most important feature of our healthcare system, the most likely response is the hospital. And they would be right: hospitals are the epicenter of our healthcare system. But if you ask them if they look forward to their next hospital visit, they would think you were insane. We dislike them and fear them, but we know nothing else. We take them for granted, and never think of an alternative. We have been conditioned to think of healthcare as acute care. The notion that the focus of healthcare could be on prevention (in all its forms), not just on cures, is an alien concept. But it is one we should quickly accept, and for which we should strive. We are conditioned to equate healthcare with acute care. And yet …

- Who wants to be sick and have to see a physician?
- Who in his or her right mind would want to be a "patient," defined as someone who suffers long and long endures?
- Who wouldn't avoid admission to a hospital if they possibly could? Who in their right mind would actually choose to be a patient in a hospital?
- And what normal person would want to go to an emergency department for non-emergency medical care?

Most of us will develop medical problems of one kind or another, and in the absence of any other recourse, some of us will be forced to visit an emergency room. Some of us will need hospital care. And some of us will indeed have to suffer long, even with that care. But none of us want any of these more than we need to. We want to minimize our contact with the healthcare system—and rightfully so. Who likes hospital visits? Even worse, hospital stays?

So in today's medical environment, we should expect a delivery system capable of helping us avoid as many of these undesirable outcomes as possible. Our system isn't capable. And those of us who live with complex and chronic medical conditions should expect the delivery system to be able to help us avoid as many hospital admissions, emergency room visits, and physician visits as possible. And ideally, the system should help us remain as active as possible.

In Chapter Three, we introduced you to four broad categories that make up the total healthcare population (illustrated in the diagram below).

- The top box describes the general population—everyone living within the nation's borders. For the bulk of the population, healthcare is not a major issue—most of the population is in relatively good health, and so long as we are in good health, we don't think about healthcare.

- Within the general population there is a significant segment that may not have a chronic condition, but they are seriously at risk of succumbing to one (the second box). Alcoholics may not suffer from liver issues, but at some point they will. Obesity doesn't immediately generate diabetes, but at some point it inevitably does.

- Once the condition takes hold, those at risk move into the third box. At this point, the current healthcare system accommodates them and kicks into high gear. Before this point, the at-risk population is of little interest to healthcare providers. It is not until they move from risk to reality that the money flows.

The Misguided Focus of Current Health Care Delivery

In the current healthcare system, then, the focus is on the bottom two boxes. It has no interest in the top two boxes, because it has no incentive to do so. The rewards are in the bottom two boxes.

Instead of a healthcare system that promotes and responds to sickness and ill-health, we need a system that promotes health and prevents ill-health and that still cares for those who become ill. We need a system that pulls as many people as possible out of the box at the bottom and places them in the box above it. And we don't want the system to stop there: wherever it can, we want the system to take as many people as possible from the second box from the bottom and put them in the box above it … and better yet, take as many as people as possible from the at-risk population and put them back into the general population.

That should be the purpose of healthcare delivery, (as suggested in the diagram below) which also suggests the broad brush strokes of a plan to improve healthcare and the health of people without adding more money into the healthcare delivery system:

- Start with a focus on those that are most sick and the most costly (the bottom two blocks in the diagram)—those with chronic medical conditions, those needing the most attention, and those who are hospitalized and suffer avoidable complications and side effects—and provide a relentless focus on improving medical practice so that patient care is accomplished without needless tests, drugs, and procedures.
- Apply the money saved to improving the health of the rest of the population (the two blocks at the top of the diagram). By improving healthcare delivery (bottom two blocks) we can improve the health of the population (top two blocks).

A Healthier Focus for Health Care Delivery

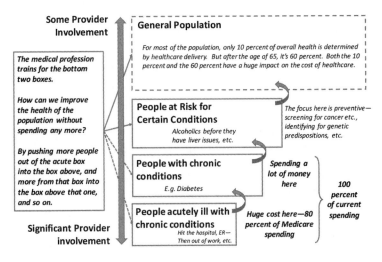

The result will be a deliberately designed system that produces improved outcomes, greater safety, better service, and a higher functional status for every individual within the general public.

The Power of Value

Shifting healthcare delivery to the kind of system described above represents a profound change of focus, and more than that—a profound shift of mind-set. But what will drive that shift? One thing more than any other: a purpose shaped by a focus on *value*. At the heart of that mind-set shift is a focus on value.

Now if "value" as a purpose sounds nebulous or even anti-climactic, don't dismiss it too quickly. It is a very powerful concept. If we could sum up in one word what healthcare needs, that would be it: *value* ... value in healthcare delivery. The purpose of the healthcare delivery system is to provide value to the patient—not only to the sick, but also to the entire population (present and future patients)—which needs to operate in a system that offers unquestionable value. The goal is a high-value healthcare delivery system—a system that produces better results at lower cost. That's what we mean by "value."

Let's unpack it.

What do we mean by "value"? Value is both disarmingly simple and surprisingly complex. We define value as a function of quality and cost—as expressed in the equation below. We achieve value when the quality is greater than the cost of the delivery—not for a single intervention, but over the span of the care cycle.

Value = Quality (Outcomes, Safety, Service) ÷ **Total Cost** (Over a Span of Care)

Total cost in this equation is measured at multiple levels: it reflects total spending over time for a patient, a condition, a population, or a payer.

What do we mean by quality? Quality covers multiple elements: better clinical outcomes, greater safety, and more efficient service. Other parameters reflect quality including fewer complications, less rework, faster return to work or functionality, and higher productivity ("readiness" in military terms). Productivity, by the way, covers every economic and demographic sphere, whether individual, employee, workforce, military, or student productivity. If the healthcare system is delivering this kind of quality (at a lower cost), we have indeed created value.

As we contemplate this future state we are striving for, it's important to remember that our focus is on actual results—outcomes, safety, service and costs. The future state should be higher-value healthcare: that is, improved quality at lower spending. So at the level of the entire healthcare system, the primary focus is on actual results (outcomes, safety, service, and costs) rather than on inputs and compliance with processes. That doesn't let individual delivery organizations off the hook from monitoring their internal processes and inputs to produce better outcomes, better safety, and better service—in addition to eliminating waste. In fact, to accomplish the vision for healthcare, it requires them to do so—all organizations need to relentlessly monitor their actual results to make sure that their processes of care are indeed reaching the ultimate goal of improved value in healthcare.

Such a high-value healthcare delivery system has implications that are at odds with much in our current delivery system. And that is why it is so difficult to secure the much-needed change. This future state we are striving towards is characterized by …

- *Cost not being the primary determinant in selecting treatment.* Value is. That means that to improve the health of the population or an at-risk segment of the population, we would opt for a more expensive test or treatment at a particular stage of diagnosis and treatment if it produces better results and/or lowers total spending over the span of the care. That kind of clinical decision-making is currently not a priority in our current system.
- *Payment made for results and outcomes (in other words, value)—not for process or compliance.* Our current payment system, by contrast, requires no accountability for results—only for compliance with regulatory and process reporting requirements.
- *Success measured by illness prevented, not by illness treated.* Prevention and health are the cornerstones of the healthcare system—not acute care. In this future state, a hospitalization of a patient, especially any one that

is avoidable, is viewed as a failure of the system. Also, hospitals are not the apex of the system ... in stark contrast to the current system, where the implicit goal of healthcare delivery is to respond to the ill-health of the population, and where the well-being of the medical profession is founded on the pervasiveness of illness: the more sick the population, the better off the medical profession.

- *The medical profession being animated by a very different aspiration.* This is a huge shift! Success in this paradigm means that doctors see visits decrease. They will see surgeries decrease. Are they ready for that?

- *Health being promoted and healthcare delivered through an engineered system* that provides high-quality, affordable healthcare for everyone.

- *Healthcare as a system is dynamic, learning, innovative, and responsive—* and places the patient firmly at the center of focus.

So what are we looking for? *Value.* It may sound simplistic, but it's powerful.

||||||||||||||||||||||||||||||||||||||||||||||||||||||||||||||||||||||||||||||||||||||||||||||||||||||||||||||||||||||||||||||

The purpose of healthcare is to provide the patient with *value*—better outcomes at lower cost.

||||||||||||||||||||||||||||||||||||||||||||||||||||||||||||||||||||||||||||||||||||||||||||||||||||||||||||||||||||||||||||||

And *that* is the purpose of healthcare: to provide the patient with *value*— which means better outcomes at lower cost.

Redefining the Relationship among the Five Domains

If the stakeholders in healthcare embraced this singular purpose (value), it would radically reconfigure the healthcare landscape. Instead of the five domains competing as a cacophonous orchestra, we would experience healthcare synchronized by a common purpose and a common vision.

In Chapter Two, we described the existing relationship among these five domains, as they currently exist today. If you remember, it looks like this:

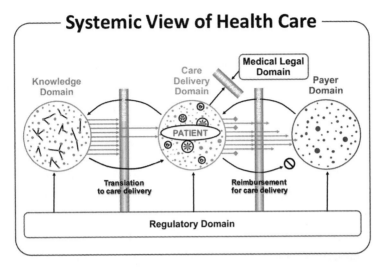

These five domains are disconnected, separated by elaborate interfaces acting as filters that introduce a significant degree of dysfunction whenever the domains try to connect and interact.

What would it look like if we could reconfigure these domains to unite in the pursuit of a common purpose for healthcare? How would the different domains relate to each other and interface with each other? If we could reconfigure the interplay and interdependence of these five domains, it would look more like the diagram below.

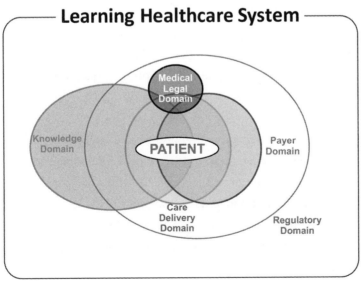

Notice just how different these two diagrams are:

- In the first diagram, the patient is at the center of the diagram in lip service only. All the other domains are linearly arranged. The regulators, subject to congressional influence, have an outsized influence on the interfaces between the circles—producing a distortion that only encourages the parties on either side of the interface to fight for control. The result is that the various sectors work to maximize their own interests, not to optimize the output of the entire system.

- The second diagram is strikingly different, because the *system* is dramatically different. The patient is truly at the center. No one wins if the patient does not receive high-value care—timely, effective, efficient care, the first time, and every time. The regulatory domain's role becomes one of facilitating and measuring results and setting standards of behavior and interaction, clarifying expectations for the best care based on the performance of the best delivery organizations, and making sure that reimbursement is linked to actual outcomes in terms of safety, service, and the functional health of individuals. And all of this is accomplished with an atmosphere of continuous learning by all sectors involved.

The implications of such a different delivery system are huge. The result would be a redistribution of attention and priority that would recognize the following realities:

- The knowledge domain will always be the largest. Its goal is to bring the research it generates into the care delivery domain, so that the care delivery domain becomes more effective, thereby providing the patient with value—better outcomes at lower cost.

- The relationship between the care delivery domain and the payer domain is a critical one. The greater the alignment and overlap between the two, the better.

- The critical task of the payer domain is to align incentives and payments so that the care delivery domain provides the patient with value—better outcomes at lower cost.

- The reach of the regulatory domain is huge. Regulators can play a vital role in several key ways by:

  o Promulgating the vision and goals.

  o Setting expectations for results and costs based on actual results attained by the best providers.

  o Ensuring transparency of outcomes, safety, service and costs. The healthcare delivery system must become an open and transparent learning system, absorbing all it can from all the inevitable complications, side effects, mistakes, and near misses, whether or not these events enter the legal domain. The regulatory domain can help facilitate this evolution.

  o Monitoring the system to eliminate abuse.

  o Avoiding the temptation to confuse oversight with micromanagement—perhaps its greatest challenge. The regulatory domain's function is to free the system to provide the patient and the country with value in healthcare delivery and health (better outcomes at lower cost), without abdicating its role of oversight.

- And finally, a healthy system requires a positive overlap between the legal domain with the care delivery and knowledge domains. It is important that patients receive appropriate recompense for malpractice events. It is equally important, however, that these events become known and analyzed within a learning organizational environment.

In Review

What, then, is the purpose of healthcare? It is to provide the patient with value—better outcomes at lower cost. The purpose of healthcare is to be patient–focused. With a focus on the patient, healthcare delivery will:

- Provide the best results through outstanding healthcare delivery and through basic, clinical and applied research.

- And at the same time promote relentless learning from all that we do for and to patients by sharing learning throughout the whole system.

Which leads us to our next question ... what will *that* look like?
What kind of vision does that give us for healthcare?
That is the subject of our next chapter.

Chapter 6

What Should Be Our Vision for Heathcare?

The Power of Vision

V ision is powerful. Every decision you make is easier and clearer with a sense of where you want to go, what you want to achieve, and what it will look like when you have achieved it. As the late Stephen Covey once said, "It's much easier to say 'no' when you have a higher 'yes.'"

In the previous chapter, we focused on the purpose of healthcare. We presented an analysis of the current delivery system and offered a viewpoint of what a future system could and should look like—at least in terms of its purpose. That purpose points the way to what healthcare delivery could look like in more concrete terms—in other words, a *vision* for healthcare.

However we describe that vision, the transition to the new reality in healthcare delivery requires something of critical importance: a good supply of visionary leaders who lead with and from a clear sense of purpose. Sometimes visionary leadership is perceived as dictatorial leadership, but the truth is that success depends on the persistent pursuit of a *shared* vision, embraced not just by the leaders, but also by those they lead. As their people take ownership of the vision, they collectively work to sustain that vision with passion, discipline, courage, persistence, and creativity, and as they do so, their efforts become contagious. So with this in mind, this chapter focuses on the kind of vision that mobilizes the greatest number of present and future leaders for a successful transformation of healthcare.

Such vision is not limited to theory. Performance numbers actually bear out the power of a vision as well. A Harvard study, conducted by John Kotter and Jim Heskett with 207 companies in 22 industries over 11 years worldwide, found that companies with vision-led cultures significantly outperformed those without one, and this translated into four key performance criteria described in the table below.

COMPANIES WITH VISION-LED CULTURES OUTPERFORMED THOSE WITHOUT ONE

	WITH	*WITHOUT*
1. Increased Revenue	682%	166%
2. Expanded Workforce	282%	36%
3. Growth of Share Price	901%	74%
4. Improved Net Income	756%	1%

Kotter and Heskett, 1992

207 companies in 22 industries over 11 years, worldwide

On every count, the difference between organizations with a clear vision and those without one is striking and compelling, and with every metric, the difference becomes even starker ... it's hard to argue against a metric that reflects a downright staggering 756% difference between the two. If ever anyone needed some compelling numbers for the power of vision, they are right here.

There is plenty more research that underscores the power of vision14. Companies like Nordstrom, Sony, Disney, Marriott, Wal-Mart, the Mayo Clinic and a good many others have demonstrated a long and sustained performance, high value, and strong customer loyalty. Such companies are driven by a vision, rooted in strong core values and a deep sense of purpose, which goes far beyond

---

14   See, for example, Jerry Porras and Jim Collins' research in *Built to Last*, one of the most enduring examples of such research.

just making money. For instance, in the case of Disney, it even went as far as creating an entire language to reinforce the company's vision: employees are "cast members," customers are "guests," and jobs are "parts" in a "performance." For the Mayo Clinic, its core value of "the needs of the patient coming first" was so strong that it solidified the culture and raised the vision and values to a cult-like status.

For such companies, their values and their vision unite and hold them together. Under stress, they default to these deeply held core values and this widely embraced vision. On this solid rock of values and vision, they make decisions that are in the best interests of the company. They provide stability and continuity, even when the company has to adjust its strategies and structures to keep competing successfully in a climate of rapid change. Vision is powerful.

The Power of Vision: an Example from the Federal Government

A clear and compelling vision can bring clarity to even the most complex of circumstances. Mergers are particularly complex, and are often derailed because the vision of either becomes the vision of neither, and the new entity operates in a vacuum.

If mergers are difficult in the private sector, they are doubly so within the Federal Government, where so many constituencies have to be won over and enlisted. And yet in 2012, the US Department of the Treasury engineered a remarkable merger between two bureaus—the Bureau of Public Debt and the Bureau of Financial Management Services—combining them into a new bureau called "Fiscal Service."

The consolidation of the two bureaus was a textbook case of a well-led consolidation, and one of the most effective tools in that consolidation was the articulation of a well-defined and compelling vision. David Lebryk, the Commissioner of the former Financial Management Service bureau and the first Commissioner of the new entity, took the opportunity of the consolidation to clarify and define the mission and vision for Fiscal Service—or more accurately, to lead a debate that resulted in a clear articulation of both their mission and vision. The mission they defined is as follows: "We exist to promote the financial integrity and operational efficiency of the US government through exceptional accounting, borrowing, collections, payments, and shared services."

Their vision was summarized in a simple, but audacious goal: "We will transform financial management and the delivery of shared services in the federal government." Particularly interesting were the details they brought to that vision, which is worth sharing in full:

Fiscal Service will be known as the entity that helped transform the way the government manages its finances and delivers shared services. We will introduce a level of efficiency, transparency, and accountability that positively affects the public perception of how government works. Fiscal Service will be a catalyst in the transformation of the federal government, demonstrating a deep commitment to serving the interests of the American people and the agencies we serve. We will be driven by a passion for improving financial management and shared service delivery through our own efficient and effective operations and through our guidance and assistance to others. We will lead and support, not simply process and account.

While never losing focus on our critical program responsibilities— essential to the operation of the federal government—we will use our proven ability to perform and our strengths to make government better.

Fiscal Service will become a sought-after resource. We will be a valued partner for agencies as they work to strengthen their own financial management or as they look for a quality service provider who can allow them to focus on their missions. We will not only provide exceptional service, but we will also collaborate with and help other organizations raise the level of their performance. We will not only collect and manage data, but we will also make it understandable and available for agencies to improve program effectiveness. When we exercise our authority, we will do so in partnership with those we direct.

Fiscal Service will be the place where people most want to work in the federal government. We will be known as both a challenging and rewarding place to work, and an organization recognized for developing experts and leaders. Working at Fiscal Service will be a credential in its own right, will carry a special prestige in the federal government, and will thus enable us to recruit the best talent in the marketplace. Our employees and organization will be the hallmark of ethical and values-based behavior. How we do our work will be as important as what we do.

At Fiscal Service we know that...

- *What we do is important,*
- *What we do makes a difference, and*
- *What we do, we do well.*

The articulation of this vision won over many, and in so doing, it became not only a vision for Fiscal Service, but a *shared* vision for Fiscal Service.

Incidentally, it also quickly produced some striking financial results. Through the shared services it offers (a quasi-outsourcing service, internal to the government), in one case alone, it generated over $250 million in savings for a platform upgrade by orchestrating the upgrade for over 30 agencies rather than each agency managing its own upgrade ... for an agency cost of $275,000 instead of the seven to eight million dollar cost per agency had each one managed its own upgrade (or given up in the attempt). Not only is a clear vision engaging; it invariably justifies itself economically.

Vision and Healthcare

When we have a vision for something, we imagine what it will look like at some point in the future ... we *see* it, at least in our imagination. Someone once observed that everything goes through two creations: first in the mind of the creator as a concept, and a second time in its actual creation or execution.

Vision is future. It describes something that hasn't happened, but that you hope to see happen. It's that point on the horizon you are moving towards and striving for. Whatever the terrain, you keep moving towards that point. You could have picked any number of points on the horizon—but you picked that particular one, and on that particular one you focus.

So what is that particular point on the horizon we are striving towards in healthcare?

The Institute of Medicine has written one of the best vision statements we have seen for the kind of healthcare environment we would all like to see established:

> *Our vision is for a healthcare system that draws on the best evidence to provide the care most appropriate to each patient, emphasizes prevention and health promotion, delivers the best value, adds to learning throughout the delivery of care, and leads to improvements in the nation's health.*[15]

Notice the five components:

1. Applying the best available medical information to the specific needs of a particular patient
2. Emphasizing prevention and health promotion
3. Delivering the best value
4. Making widely available the experience gained through healthcare delivery
5. Leading to improvement in the nation's health.

The Institute goes further by offering a concrete goal:

> "By the year 2020, 90 percent of clinical decisions will be supported by accurate, timely, and up-to-date clinical information, and will reflect the best available evidence."[16]

That goal has the hallmarks of a "BHAG"—a big, hairy, audacious goal. It's big enough to get our attention, and realistic enough to garner our commitment. So with that in mind, let's take a more detailed look at the preferred vision for healthcare.

---

15   *The Learning Healthcare System*, Institute of Medicine, page ix.
16   Idem.

The Vision: Value and Access

If we were to synthesize these thoughts, we would frame the vision as *high-quality, affordable healthcare for everyone*. This vision has two components:

1. Value—High quality that is affordable
2. Access—Available for everyone

Access for everyone means universal coverage. This may sound like a partisan political agenda. It isn't. That's not to say that it doesn't have political implications; clearly it does. But its political implications are bipartisan. It is in fact a bipartisan imperative that, for different reasons, both sides of the political spectrum can embrace. For one side, it is an issue of fairness and compassion, and for the other, it is an economic imperative for high-value, low-cost healthcare. Both sides should see their political priorities satisfied in the pursuit of universal healthcare coverage. It's important for those to the right, those traditionally most vociferously opposed to universal coverage, to understand that it doesn't eliminate competition. In fact, to work effectively, it *requires* competition, and the market's offering of a range of insurance options expresses that competition. As Elizabeth Teisberg,[17] a leading champion for high-value healthcare points out, "universal coverage doesn't equal socialized medicine."[18] She cites Europe as an example, where …

"… different countries achieve universal coverage with a variety of approaches: single payer, multi-payer, and individual payers with subsidies; with and without direct involvement of employers; with varying percentages of physicians paid by the government, by hospitals, or in private practice; with government and private hospitals—sometimes competing; with varying degrees of local and national involvement in

---

17   Elizabeth Teisberg is currently a professor in the Dartmouth Center for Healthcare Delivery Science, as well as a Senior Institute Associate at Harvard's Institute for Strategy and Competitiveness.
18   Elizabeth Teisberg, HBR Blog Network, *Healthcare Reform Is Good for Business*, June 29, 2012

funding; and with different budgeting approaches, different ranges of available services, and different lengths of wait for care."[19]

The fact is that universal coverage already exists in America: anyone without insurance will not be turned away by a hospital. But that is a very expensive and inefficient way to provide universal coverage—not only because treatment isn't addressed with an intentional and planned response to prevent recurrence of hospital admissions and emergency visits, but also because it delays intervention to a point where the intervention is much more expensive and the outcome is much less certain.

So the economic argument for universal healthcare is strong and compelling, and true to form in economic theory and practice, its absence has created a dysfunctional system that keeps raising the cost of healthcare without improving its quality. When insurance coverage is unavailable for pre-existing conditions, when insurance premiums are increased with ill-health, and when low-income families and working people cannot afford healthcare insurance, the economic unintended consequences are significant and profoundly negative: costs increase and quality deteriorates.

Again, access for all does not eliminate competition. To work effectively, access for all will require competition, and it will need to be market-based. However, access for all is not the magic bullet for healthcare. It is an important condition, but for high-quality, affordable healthcare for everyone to become a reality, it will require something more: it will require a firmly established, well-functioning learning system that facilitates the kind of healthcare delivery we have been describing. It will do little good to provide everyone access to a healthcare system that is inefficient, low quality, wasteful, and unnecessarily expensive.

Summary

If we were to summarize the key ideas we have covered so far, it would look something like this:

---

19   Idem

- Healthcare needs to be focused on the needs of the patient—not on the interests of any of the particular healthcare stakeholders.
- High-value healthcare delivery is the purpose of healthcare.
- Provider payment must be linked to value.
- All citizens should be expected to have basic health insurance, at least for catastrophic events, while preserving patient choice.
- Healthcare needs to operate as a learning system, where stakeholders self-organize in such a way that high-value care is the result.
- Leadership is the critical ingredient for change—leadership at all levels and in every domain of healthcare. Without it, the reformation and transformation we all want to see in healthcare will never happen.

We clarified the purpose of healthcare and proposed a vision for its future in this chapter and the preceding one. But how will this be operationalized? Read on for the answer to this important question.

Chapter 7

How Should Healthcare Be Organized?

To paraphrase Peter Drucker, at some point all great ideas and lofty aspirations have to "degenerate into action." In our journey to the reformation of the healthcare industry, it's time to articulate that "degeneration."

Execution and action in any organization are about systems—harnessing the systems to give impetus to mission and vision. In healthcare, it's not just about any system—it's about a *learning* system—an overall national learning system as well as a multitude of organizations within healthcare that act as learning organizations.

This picture of an overall learning system, containing many learning healthcare organizations, captures an important feature of the future state we are looking for in healthcare. In his book *The Fifth Discipline: The Art and Practice of The Learning Organization (1990)*, Peter Senge defined a learning organization as one "where people continually expand their capacity to create the results they truly desire, where new and expansive patterns of thinking are nurtured, where collective aspiration is set free, and where people are continually learning to see the whole together." Expressed differently, a learning system or a learning organization is as a system where everyone in the system knows what the collective system knows.

The Importance of a Learning System

Much has been written about learning organizations. And it is all relevant: hospitals and care-provider systems need to be learning organizations. Doctors, nurses, and administrators should operate within a learning organization. But we need more than that: we need not just learning organizations—we need a learning *system*. We need healthcare as a whole to be a learning system—which means that everyone in the system knows what the system knows.

What do we mean by a "system"? Systems are everywhere. Great leaders understand systems. They recognize their importance, and they learn how to lead within them and through them ... and sometimes despite them. For some leadership roles, systems thinking is critical, but for all, it is important. If your leadership role is primarily operational, understanding systems thinking is essential.

Systems thinking is a relatively recent discipline. Barry Richmond first used the term "systems thinking" in the late 1980s. In a paper delivered at the 1994 International Systems Dynamics Conference in Sterling, Scotland he defined systems thinking as "the art and science of making reliable inferences about behavior by developing an increasingly deep understanding of underlying structure."[20]

The discipline took a significant step forward when Peter Senge, founding chair of the Society for Organizational Learning and a senior lecturer at MIT, published *The Fifth Discipline*[21]. With his focus on learning organizations, he defined systems thinking as an approach to problem solving that views an "unintended consequence" as a result or outcome of the interactions of *all* the components of an overall system, rather than the result of a single or isolated portion or component of that system.

For much of the last century, organizations were viewed as essentially mechanistic entities that could be directly controlled and shaped. Pull one lever

---

20 http://www.iseesystems.com/resources/Articles/SDSTletsjustgetonwithit.pdf.
21 *The Fifth Discipline*, one of the most complete and thorough analyses of systems thinking.

and you get one result; pull another and you get a different one. After World War II, people began to look at organizations as more fluid organisms, where growth and development were for the most part invisible and largely undetected. By the end of the century, systems thinking had become a powerful and significant tool in understanding organizational behavior—and a powerful and significant tool for leaders in shaping organizational behavior.[22]

The Pervasiveness of Systems

Systems thinking as a discipline may be relatively recent, but systems themselves are as old as the universe. The solar system, for example, is made up of a multitude of interacting parts and is itself part of a much larger galactic system. Our bodies are made up of different systems—we have a nervous system, a digestive system, a skeletal system, and they all interact with each other. When we travel, we are at the mercy of changing weather systems, which may so dramatically disrupt the air traffic system that we completely miss our connections, which may in turn do a number on our nervous system! We often see powerful weather systems impact economic and social systems, sometimes even severely. Social and ecological systems influence other systems and are themselves influenced by still other systems. Economic and social systems affect each other, and both are moved by sub-systems within each one. The examples are limitless: systems can be as small as the DNA system or as large as the galactic system.

And, of course, an organization is a system. A business is a system, a government agency is a system, a non-profit organization is a system, an orchestra is a system, and an academic institution is a system. Even a department is a system. And a whole industry—such as healthcare—is a system. It may be very dysfunctional, it may perform very poorly, it may be unplanned and chaotic, and it may be self-destructing as a system, but it still remains a system.

Systems are indeed everywhere. We live and operate in many different systems, and even if we're not conscious of them, they actually profoundly impact us. So to exercise great leadership, we need to understand the systems we

---

22   While system thinking is relatively recent in its current form, its origins go back at least as far as the 1920s with the introduction of Statistical Process Control, and it is built on the tradition of Deming, TQM (Total Quality Management), BPR (Business Process Reengineering), and Six Sigma—all different manifestations of systems thinking.

operate in and shape them to provide the best delivery of the service our purpose, vision and values drive us to deliver.

Systems Thinking and Leadership

Systems are about interdependence. They create linkages far stronger than we may even realize. They create interactions, sequences, and relationships. They bring together different interrelated forces so that, in one way or another, everything affects everything else.

Systems thinking as a discipline recognizes the importance of these systems. Recognizing their importance allows us to not only anticipate the ripple effect of every choice we make and every initiative we undertake, but also allows us to shape and direct the systems in our organization—and in our industry—so that they reinforce rather than hinder the direction we are pursuing. That happens because leaders make it happen.

Organizations are not just a function of the boxes in the organizational chart, with names in the boxes and appropriate lines connecting the boxes to each other. Organizations are just as much a function of what happens in between the boxes, and in reality, what happens between the boxes is usually more significant than what happens inside the boxes … unless the people in the boxes know how to influence what happens in between the boxes.

And that's a leadership issue. As the late Michael Hammer, author and MIT professor, put it, "Fixing the pieces of a process won't solve the larger problem … yet … management works at fixing the pieces instead of redesigning the processes by which the company's work gets done." In other words, it is the job of leadership to improve the way the work gets done, and leaders do so by focusing on the whole, not just on the pieces. W. Edwards Deming, a thought-leader in developing, applying, and teaching a systems-thinking approach to improving the effectiveness and efficiency of organizations, underscored the importance of leadership: "Institute leadership. The aim of leadership should be to help people, machines and gadgets do a better job."

Leadership matters, then, because, knowingly or unknowingly, leaders shape systems, and they shape the systems of the organization either to reinforce or to hinder its aspirations. And more than just at an organizational level, the leaders throughout an entire industry (such as healthcare) can influence and shape the systems that make up that industry.

Systems thinking is a function of values and core beliefs. Values shape systems, and shaping those values is a leadership function. Although Deming didn't call it as such, in essence he was teaching values. As a recap, here are the values and core beliefs we identified at the end of the previous chapter:

- Healthcare needs to be focused on the needs of the patient—not on the interests of any particular healthcare stakeholders.
- High-value healthcare delivery is the purpose of healthcare.
- Providers must be paid for value.
- All citizens should be expected to have basic health insurance at least for catastrophic events, while preserving patient choice.
- Healthcare needs to operate as a learning system, where stakeholders self-organize in such a way that high-value care is the result.
- Leadership is critical for change—leadership at all levels and in every domain of healthcare.

Whatever you value, you reward and reinforce; whatever you reward and reinforce shapes behaviors. Rewarding and reinforcing the right values and behaviors is a leadership function.

Healthcare as a System

So the vision for healthcare needs to be anchored in a learning system. One of the best descriptions of such a healthcare system was offered by the Institute of Medicine [23], which described it as follows:

Science and Information Technology

- *Real-time access to knowledge*—A learning healthcare system continuously and reliably captures, curates, and delivers the best available evidence to guide, support, tailor, and improve clinical decision-making and care, safety, and quality.

---

23 *The Learning Healthcare System:* Workshop Summary (IOM Roundtable on Evidence-Based Medicine), Institute of Medicine 2007

- *Digital capture of the care experience*—A learning healthcare system captures the care experience on digital platforms for real-time generation and application of knowledge for care improvement.

Patient-Clinician Partnerships

- *Engaged, empowered patients*—A learning healthcare system is anchored on patient needs and perspectives and promotes the inclusion of patients, families, and other caregivers as vital members of the continuously learning care team.

Incentives

- *Incentives aligned for value*—In a learning healthcare system, incentives are actively aligned to encourage continuous improvement, identify and reduce waste, and reward high-value care.

- *Full Transparency*—A learning healthcare system systematically monitors the safety, quality, processes, prices, costs, and outcomes of care, and makes information available for care improvement and informed choices and decision-making by clinicians, patients, and their families.

Culture

- *Leadership-instilled culture of learning*—A learning healthcare system is stewarded by leaders at all levels committed to a culture of teamwork, collaboration, and adaptability in support of continuous learning as a core aim.

- *Supportive system competencies*—In a learning healthcare system, complex care operations and processes are constantly refined through ongoing team training and skill building, systems analysis and information development, and creation of the feedback loops for continuous learning and system improvement.

That's a pretty good description of what a healthy healthcare system would look like. But we aren't there yet. How, then, do we implement it?

The Six Elements of a Healthy Healthcare System

A healthy healthcare learning system moves us from data to wisdom. Data is simply random facts, by themselves of little use. But if that data is translated into useful information about a patient, it can become knowledge about a group of patients, which allows us to make wise and sensible decisions for all parties involved.

Data ➔ Information (About the Patient) ➔ Knowledge (About Groups of Patients) ➔ Wisdom in Healthcare Delivery

For such a learning system to exist, and for organizations within such a system to be genuine learning organizations, it requires the presence of six critical elements:

1. Focus on Value
2. Pay for Value
3. Insurance for All
4. Integration and Coordination
5. Delivery System Optimization
6. Individualized Medicine

These six critical elements are captured in the diagram below.

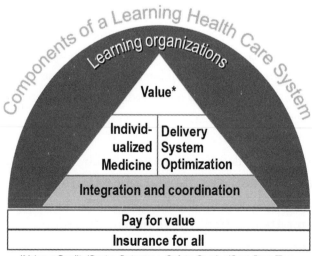

*Value = Quality/Cost = Outcomes, Safety, Service/Cost Over Time

The Foundation and the Capstone

In the diagram above, the two elements of the foundation were addressed in previous chapters—*Pay for Value* was addressed in Chapter Five (the Purpose of Healthcare) and *Insurance for All* was addressed in Chapter Six (the Vision for Healthcare).

We also addressed *Value*—the capstone in this pyramid—in Chapter Five. By way of reminder, we defined value with the following equation:

Value = Quality (Outcomes, Safety, Service) / Total Cost (Over a Span of Care)

In this equation:

- **Quality** is defined by patient outcomes (such as patient mortality rates, faster return to work or functionality, readmission), safety (such as fewer complications, less rework), and service (such as access to care, patient satisfaction).
- **Total Cost** refers to the spending over a defined time for a particular patient, condition or population.

So there you have the foundation and the capstone. The remaining three elements need some explanation.

Integration and Coordination

Integration refers to the way the providers communicate, collaborate, and function as a team with the patient as the center of their efforts. It is the way care providers and their decisions are integrated for the benefit of the patient.

Coordination refers to the way actual medical care delivery is orchestrated for the patient—in the hospital, laboratory, procedure room, operating room, ER, medical clinic, nursing home, the patient's home, the patient's school, the patient's work, or wherever the patient happens to be. Someone has to be the conductor for this complicated orchestra. Today this function frequently falls to a family member—the mother, father, daughter, or son. In the future, skilled and dedicated providers assisting the patients and their families will much better accomplish this overwhelming responsibility.

Delivery System Optimization

Optimizing the healthcare delivery system has two components:

- *Systems engineering*—which is focused on the processes within healthcare, whether medical or administrative. An operation is a process, and so is billing. Systems engineering analyzes these processes, and typically those engaged in the process are the best placed to improve it. A group of surgeons, for example, decided to help with cleaning and sanitizing the operating rooms between operations and so reduced the total time by ten minutes—which over multiple operations in the course of a day, proved to be a substantial improvement. This concept includes patient-centric workflow design in medical clinics, imaging facilities, diagnostic testing facilities, ERs, operating rooms, and any location where patient care is administered.

- *Science of healthcare delivery*—which is the systematic study of how to improve the systemic processes of care, in order to develop new models of care that produce higher quality at lower cost, and thus improve value. The science of healthcare delivery is focused on the individual, tailoring the intervention to a specific individual, and focusing on measurement of results including outcomes of care, safety, patient service and total patients costs over time.

For an optimized delivery system, these two components are indispensable.

Individualized Medicine

Individualized Medicine also has two components, closely related:

- Personalized medicine from medical advances—the application of recent medical advances to a patient's particular condition. In other words, how do we make use of novel diagnostic and therapeutic discoveries coming out of medical research and practice? These would include genetic testing, identifying and targeting proteins that affect the way that cells respond, transplantation of specific organs (e.g. for diabetes), and novel medical devices.

- Personalized medicine from existing practices—taking the active ingredients we already have and applying them effectively and efficiently to the specific needs of a specific patient.

The goal of personalized medicine has been described, appropriately, as *Prediction, Prevention, and Personalized Therapy*. The focus has been primarily on an individual patient. But what about the health of the whole population, not just the individual patient? If we want to improve the health of a population, we need to focus on improving the health of every person in that population, and the effectiveness of this kind of individualized medicine requires predicting likely health issues, working to prevent them, and personalizing the responses when they do occur. So the same concepts—*prediction, prevention, and personalized therapy*—apply just as much to the tactics we use for improving the health of the overall population.

Effective individualized medicine, then, will not only improve the condition of individual patients, it will also improve the health of the overall population.

Summary

These, then, are the six key elements of a learning system that we have just been through:

1. Pay for Value
2. Insurance for All
3. Integration and Coordination
4. Individualized Medicine
5. Delivery System Optimization
6. Focus on Value

Why are they so important? Because they give us the basic levers that enable the stakeholders to self-organize in such a way that high-value care results within a widespread and dynamic learning system.

They also give us the key skills and tactics needed to engineer this transformation, building on the current elements and infrastructure that exist today. And they give us the fundamental tactics and skills we need for this transformation:

1. *A relentless focus on value*—a relentless *leadership* focus on creating value in healthcare by measuring and monitoring performance and transparency.
2. *Coordinated care* for patients and *integration* among providers.
3. *Individualized medicine*—tailored for the needs of each individual patient, including all individuals in a designated population.
4. *Delivery-system optimization*—designing, monitoring, and improving the process of care delivery through the science of system engineering and the science of healthcare delivery.

So ... who will make this happen? The right leaders in the right place, exercising the right leadership.

That is the subject of Part III, but before we get there, we have one more question to address in understanding the transformation leaders need to lead:

What kind of culture should they create in healthcare?

That is the subject of the next chapter.

Chapter 8

What Should Be the Culture of Healthcare?

T he unique and essential function of leadership," Edgar Schein once said, "is the manipulation of culture." We may prefer the word "shaping" to "manipulation," but what he says holds true. Whether they know it or not and whether they like it or not, leaders are the primary agents in shaping the culture around them.

Just as every nation has a national culture, every organization has an organizational culture. Every organization has a "tribal scent" that distinguishes it from another. This tribal scent dictates a way of operating and defines a set of core values that shape the practices, habits, and decisions of the organization. Some of these practices and habits are conscious, but most are unconscious or even subconscious.

We can also ask, can a whole sector have a culture? It may seem pretentious to claim it can, especially for a sector such as healthcare, where different domains have very different cultures and where different organizations within a single domain have very different subcultures. The culture of the medical legal domain is very different from the culture of the knowledge domain and both are very different from the culture of the payer domain. Within the care-delivery domain, hospitals have different cultures from specialized clinics, and hospitals themselves have different cultures one from another. For example, Johns Hopkins is very different from Mayo Clinic, and both are very different from the VA hospital system.

But despite such differences, whole sectors can still have, and do have, a distinctive look and feel that differentiate them from other sectors. The automotive industry has a certain flavor that makes it very different from, for instance, the utility industry.

Most important is that whatever the culture, it can be shaped and influenced—including healthcare. But before we explore how it can be shaped, we need to peel back some layers on culture itself … and for starters, we need to define it: What exactly *is* culture?

The Components of Culture

Culture is often viewed as a nebulous, opaque concept, too glibly used, too easily misunderstood, and too abusively applied.

As we previously suggested, culture is the term we use to describe the environment, style, and mood of an organization. It describes, "the way we get things done here." It captures the sum total of all the aspirations, norms, rites, rituals, and rules (unwritten as well as written)—held sometimes consciously but mostly unconsciously—that make up the psychological, social, political, and moral personality of the organization, the sector or the population.

Sometimes culture is healthy, and sometimes it is not. Hence all the talk about "changing the culture." And that's where much of the confusion comes from. We don't actually change the culture. We change the things that in turn change the culture.

Culture is like the temperature around us. It may be just right, in which case we don't think about it. It may be too hot (or too cold), and we may not realize how uncomfortable it is until the temperature moves to a level we find comfortable. Or we may be very conscious that it is too hot or too cold and we need to do something about it. That's when we misguidedly talk about changing the temperature; we don't actually change the temperature any more than we change the culture. We look for the thermostat and change the setting, which in due course changes the temperature. When that occurs, we didn't change the temperature—the thermostat did.

Similarly, *we* don't change the culture. It's the thermostat that changes the culture.

So for the purposes of our discussion, what is the "thermostat"?

The thermostat can be best understood by the dials that comprise it. Fortunately, the dials on the thermostat are not numerous. In fact, to transform a culture, you need to focus on only seven critical dials:

1. The *purpose* and *direction* the organization is pursuing (its mission and vision).
2. The *values* it chooses to shape *behavior.*
3. The *focus* it adopts to define success (the *Critical Success Factors* and the *goals* it sets).
4. The way it *recruits* and *develops* its people—how it optimizes recruitment and development.
5. The organizational *systems* and *structures* it develops—how it optimizes systems and structures.
6. The process it adopts for its *execution.*
7. The kind of *leadership* it promotes.

When you as a leader adjust the settings on these dials, you move the needle on the culture—whatever its size, scope, and purpose may be.

These seven "dials" of the culture thermostat are illustrated in the diagram on the next page.

This diagram underscores some important points:

- Leadership is the master dial ... it controls all the others. With the right leadership, you can change the other dials in the direction they need to be changed.
- After leadership, the most important dials are the three to the left: the direction, the values, and the focus. Particularly important are the direction and the behaviors—the mission, vision, and values. These

The Seven Elements that Shape Culture

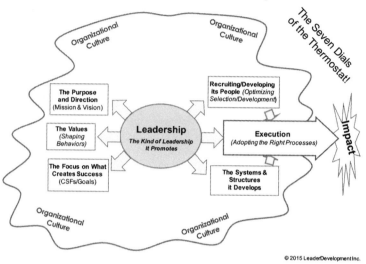

© 2015 LeaderDevelopment Inc.

are the DNA—if you know these, you understand the organization or sector.

- If you clarify the mission vision, and values, it makes it easier to identify the focus (the critical success factors and the specific goals to pursue), as well as the two dials that most immediately impact the execution: having the right people in place and the right systems and structures to support the execution.

When you have a strong and healthy culture, it's because leaders on top are constantly and vigilantly paying attention to the "temperature" of their organization. Great leaders understand the importance of organizational culture in determining organizational performance. They know where to find the thermostat and constantly monitor the dials on it. Sometimes they make significant adjustments to the readings on one or several of the dials; sometimes they fine-tune them. But whatever the dials tell them, great leaders recognize that it is their job to set the dials at the right level.

The Culture of Healthcare

These seven elements give us important guidelines for shaping culture, and in particular the culture of healthcare. We have already addressed two of the key ideas: mission and vision. We addressed the mission of healthcare in Chapter Five (*to provide the patient with value—better outcomes at lower cost*) and the vision for healthcare in Chapter Six (*high-quality, affordable healthcare for everyone*). But we haven't addressed the values.

But even before we do that, we must first consider how the mission, vision, and values work together. The diagram below illustrates how.

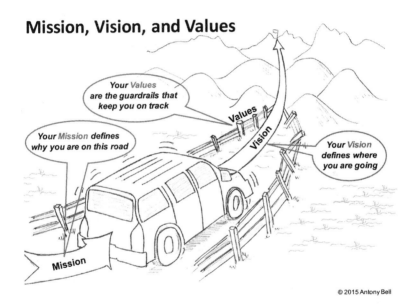

Mission, Vision, and Values

Your *Values* are the guardrails that keep you on track

Your *Mission* defines why you are on this road

Your *Vision* defines where you are going

Values

Vision

Mission

© 2015 Antony Bell

Imagine the organization (or sector) as the vehicle. The purpose or mission (the terms are interchangeable) describes why it is on this road and not another. The vision is that point on the horizon (the flag) it's aiming to get to in the future. And the values act as guard rails on the side of the road that keep the vehicle from drifting into the field on the right or the field on the left. When a decision hits up against the values, they bounce it back onto the road.

Values are, well, under-valued. We readily embrace the notion of purpose and the importance of vision, and yet ignore the task of clarifying the values—

and thereby miss a powerful tool to give both the mission and vision the highest probability of success and the highest degree of focus. In the absence of clear values, the mission and the vision themselves lose their focus. Without clear values, there is no barrier, and the vehicle drifts into the field on the right or the field on the left. It may eventually reach that flag on the horizon, but it will follow a much more circuitous route and waste a great deal more time and energy getting there.

Values are important.

The Values for Healthcare

What, then, are the critical values for healthcare? Which values are essential to pursue the purpose of providing the patient with better outcomes at a lower cost, and to fulfill the vision of high-quality, affordable healthcare for everyone?

We suggest three key values for a high-value learning healthcare system:

1. Collaboration
2. Transparency
3. Humility.

Before we expand on these, we should point out that different organizations within healthcare might have different and parallel values, which you would expect. Our point here is that if all the stakeholders within healthcare don't embrace these three in particular, there is little likelihood of fulfilling the kind of purpose and vision that otherwise generates broad buy-in.

Why these three? What do we mean by them?

Collaboration

Without collaboration, nothing will change (for the good) in healthcare. The transformation of healthcare requires and mandates collaboration. More than that, healthcare will thrive with collaboration—for the benefit of all the stakeholders involved.

The challenges in healthcare are of such magnitude that no single entity has the resources to meet them. Healthcare can only be transformed with a deep commitment to collaboration, and that collaboration needs to happen at multiple levels:

✓ Among policy makers to create a bipartisan approach
✓ Between regulators and providers
✓ Between providers and payers
✓ Between payers and regulators
✓ Between providers and healthcare educational institutions
✓ Among healthcare educational institutions
✓ Between providers and unions
✓ Between the medical legal domain and the knowledge domain
✓ Among the federal institutions within the knowledge domain
✓ Between regional care delivery systems, cooperating rather than competing ...

... to name but a few.

Collaboration at each of these levels is important, but two are crucial. If collaboration within the world of policy makers, at both a national and a regional level, can be achieved with healthcare providers, the momentum to collaborate will spread to other levels and to other areas, even to those where the absence of collaboration remains a stubborn road block to the creation of a healthcare delivery system characterized by high value—a learning system that consistently produces better results for less money over time.

Is such collaboration possible? Absolutely, and in Part IV we offer some striking examples of what has already been accomplished.

Transparency

We devoted the last chapter to the importance of a learning system. By its very nature, a learning system is transparent. Transparency is fundamental for discovering the best practices, for lowering costs, and for diffusing knowledge throughout the system. The degree to which it is transparent will be the degree to which it is a genuine learning system. Without a commitment to transparency, creating such a system will be virtually impossible.

Transparency can be applied to a number of different areas, but there is one where it must be applied: the *results* of care. When we discussed the results of care earlier, we included such measurable elements as patient outcomes, patient safety, patient satisfaction, and patient performance status (among others). Measuring and reporting results is necessary if we are to have any chance of measurably improving care for both an individual and for the system as a whole.

The results of care require two levels of transparency: internal and external. Both are critical in creating the environment where continuous learning consistently and progressively improves the results for patients.

From an internal perspective, providers can learn a great deal by simply studying the variation in results within its internal physician practices. Such variations include general outcomes, safety, complications, medical errors, utilization rates of tests and procedures, hospitalization rates, length of stay in hospital and ICU days, and quality of emergency room services. Bringing physicians to a place where they are comfortable sharing their results internally requires a change of culture, where trust and non-threatening collaboration among the staff are the hallmarks of the organization. Building such a culture is, once again, a leadership function.

If creating such internal transparency is hard enough, developing external transparency is even harder. Over the years, we have witnessed a growing reluctance to share and report results and costs outside an organization. Doctors, like other people, are reluctant to have their results known in public, especially their poor results. In addition, there are competitive and medical legal reasons for not sharing results openly. On the other hand, from a patient-care perspective (should there be any other perspective?) the benefits to mutual learning among different institutions are huge, but they require a shared vision, a deep mutual commitment, and a strong, trusting collaboration among the senior organizational leaders of the different organizations. These leaders then need the will and courage to build the same level of trust within their own staff to share information with these other external organizations. If these organizations are bound together by a common commitment to the premise that "the needs of the patient come first," such external collaborations can be remarkably successful.

It doesn't necessarily mean the end of competition. In a world where providers collaborate in the pursuit of excellent outcomes and higher levels of safety, they can still find ways to compete on service and costs.

Humility

Humility is not the kind of value we would typically think of in any marketplace context, and it needs some explanation. It isn't the same as meekness. As someone has put it, humility is not so much thinking less *of* ourselves, but thinking less *about* ourselves. As Jim Collins discovered in his *Good to Great* research, humility in the leaders of the companies he researched was reflected in a commitment to the good of the organization ahead of their own personal interests.

Defined this way, humility will be essential to genuine collaboration and widespread transparency. Humility is required for anyone to openly and squarely confront the prospect that they may not be as good as they think they are—or as good as their advertising hype projects them to be! Humility will be required of every stakeholder, because a necessary decision in the interests of the mission and vision of healthcare may run counter to the personal interests of a particular stakeholder. Every stakeholder will potentially lose something, and yet every stakeholder will likely gain much more.

For this to happen, all stakeholders will need to believe that the patient comes first, and then act accordingly. And that, after all, is what healthcare is all about.

And so it Goes ...

Here in Part II, we have proposed a purpose for healthcare, offered a vision for its future, described what healthcare would look like as a learning system, offered a way of shaping the culture of healthcare, and suggested three overarching values for healthcare (collaboration, transparency, and humility).

What would it look like if the mission, vision, and values we have described were to be widely and genuinely embraced and became part of the overall healthcare DNA? That will be the subject of later chapters. But as a glimpse into the future, we would see policy makers using the mission, vision, and values as a yardstick to measure every piece of proposed legislation. We would see regulators using a different benchmark for measuring the effectiveness of healthcare providers. We would see medical schools better equipping future physicians for a very different healthcare environment, and we would see physicians themselves embracing the importance of their contribution to this new healthcare environment.

The impact would be profound if the mission, vision, and values were to take root. In fact, healthcare would be transformed. But how would they take root? Only by the right people exercising the right leadership in the right places for the right reasons …

… which is exactly what we discuss in Part III.

PART III

The *Real* Solution:
The Right Kind of Leadership!

Is great leadership even possible in healthcare?

What do we mean by great leadership?

Why do we need a framework for great leadership?

What does great leadership look like in healthcare?

Who needs to exercise great leadership?

How?

The answers are the key to the transformation of healthcare.

Leadership matters.

Chapter 9

Why Do We Need a Framework for Great Leadership?

The Problem of Ignorance

The greatest handicap to meaningful leadership is not the absence of talent, but rather, the pervasiveness of ignorance. Most leaders do not exercise great leadership, not because they can't, but because they don't know how. They would if they only knew how.

Many leaders confuse ignorance with incapability. This sense of incapability fosters confusion and raises the wrong questions like:

Are certain personalities better suited to leadership?
What if I'm not one of them?
If I'm an introvert, can I be a great leader?
Or, if I'm an extravert, does that give me an unfair advantage?

As leaders look around at other leaders, they inevitably compare themselves to those who just seem to ooze charisma ... and the conclusions they draw are never healthy! They then begin to think: "I must be a lost cause—condemned to a life of mediocre and ineffective leadership!"

That is the wrong conclusion. Instead of incapacity or incapability, the real problem is much more likely to be ignorance: we simply don't know *how* to lead. We don't know what kind of leadership our context needs.

To understand the essentials of great leadership, it's helpful to consider what is *not* essential. This may be surprising, but charisma isn't essential, and a substantial body of research bears this out.[24] If anything, charisma is a handicap. Leaders with charisma tend to rely on their charisma alone, and ignore the qualities that really make for great leadership.

Gender does not matter either. Women have certain advantages in certain contexts, and in other contexts, men do. In either case, men and women can excel in contexts you wouldn't expect them to.

Nor is it about personality. It doesn't matter if you are an introvert, and no, you have no special advantage if you are an extrovert.

So what *is* essential to great leadership? From our perspective, two things are critical:

1. Understanding
2. Choice.

Why?
Because:

- Great leaders *understand* certain things about leadership.
- They *make certain choices* based on that understanding.

Understanding and choice drive behavior. Great leaders behave in certain ways, because the understanding they have acquired drives that behavior and the choices they have made. It is a simple formula:

UNDERSTANDING + CHOICE = BEHAVIOR

---

24 See, for example, *Built to Last,* by Jim Collins and Jerry Porras—an interesting study of enduring organizations where charisma was notably absent. The study compared these enduring companies to similar companies in the same industry that didn't do so well ... and these comparison companies were typically led by charismatic leaders.

Understanding is the starting point. If you don't understand what great leadership is, you have no chance of ever consistently exercising it. Understanding is your first priority and is the essence of great leadership.

Whatever the subject, all choices are made on our current level of understanding. We make financial choices all the time, and they may or may not be based on a sound understanding of our options. The same is true in leadership: the better our understanding, the better our choices.

Choice, too, is important. Right understanding doesn't automatically generate right choices. For all of us, there are times when we perfectly understand what we need to do, but for whatever reason, we don't make that choice. Still, without the right understanding, we would likely never make the right choice, and if we did, it would be a matter of luck and happenstance.

When we make the right choices, the right behaviors follow. No one behaves in a vacuum—every behavior is driven by a choice shaped by our understanding.

Earlier, we said that talent isn't a critical ingredient. That statement needs qualifying. Leadership is multi-faceted enough that we will inevitably find areas in which we perform better than in others. Some of us are particularly effective at defining strategies, others at executing, and others at challenging groups. Some are particularly effective at challenging an individual one on one, others at facilitating a discussion, others at creating consensus, and yet others at challenging people to think differently. In other words, each one of us has a particular type of environment in which we feel more comfortable leading.

But that doesn't mean that we can't learn to lead in situations where we are not comfortable. In fact, the areas in which we have to learn more deliberately how to lead effectively often become areas in which we do particularly well as a leader.

So, no, you are not predestined to a life of mediocre leadership! Seek out the right understanding, make the right choices, and you will exercise the right behaviors for great leadership.

If the real problem in leadership is not the absence of talent but the presence of ignorance, it is especially so in healthcare. Great leadership is not exercised, not because those who should be exercising it are willfully choosing not to, but because they don't know how to. We feel strongly that if they knew how to, they would.

The Definition of Great Leadership

To exercise great leadership, we must first define it.

How would *you* define it? If you are one of the many leaders who hasn't written out a definition, take a moment now to put a definition on paper. It's an interesting exercise. You may have done it in the past, and if you haven't, you will find it stimulating. Avoid writing a list of qualities—typically the first impulse. That's not the same as writing out a definition.

Whatever your definition, for our present purposes, we will define great leadership this way: it is *applying the right leadership to the right context for the right reason.*

Unfortunately, we lead in a complex, confusing world. As mentioned earlier, the military has coined a term to describe it: they call it a *VUCA* world … *volatile, uncertain, complex,* and *ambiguous.* Whatever our context, whatever the healthcare domain in which we operate, it's a *VUCA* world.

It makes identifying the right leadership for the right context immensely difficult. In healthcare alone, the contexts are numerous, even within one single domain of healthcare. And for every context, the solutions offered are overwhelming. As we saw in Chapter Four, leadership solutions typically involve one of the areas in the table below, and the options are overwhelming. In the face of all these options, how on earth do we know which one to choose? How do we know which is most appropriate, useful, and relevant? In Chapter Four, we identified the following daunting list of leadership qualities and skills:

- Strategic Thinking
- Competitive Advantage
- Market Analysis
- Corporate Direction and Focus
- Vision Casting
- Marketing Strategies
- Corporate Alignment
- Corporate Culture
- Corporate Life Cycles
- Critical Success Factors
- Communications Strategy
- Corporate Values Clarification
- Merger and Acquisition Integration

- Acquisition Management
- Financial Acumen
- Organizational Design
- Organizational Development
- Systems Thinking
- Business Process Reengineering
- TQM (Total Quality Management)
- Six Sigma
- Balanced Scorecard
- Transactional Leadership Operational Efficiency
- Execution
- Team Building
- Partnering
- Personal Leadership Qualities

- Moral Compass
- Self-Awareness
- Emotional Intelligence
- Relational Capacity
- Use of Assessment Instruments
- Succession Planning
- Performance Management
- Talent Selection
- Talent Development
- Leadership Development
- Coaching
- Mentoring
- Motivation
- Situational Leadership
- Delegation
- Empowerment

For many leaders, the complexity is overwhelming. Instead of applying the right leadership to the right context, they default to a one-dimensional leadership.

The Problem of One-Dimensional Leadership

I (Antony) am a runner. Well, sort of a runner. Well, used to be sort of a runner. Up until a few years ago, I was running about three times a week, between 4 and 5 miles a time. My goal was to clock more than 50 miles a month, with a pace of less than eight minutes per mile. Seven minutes, fifty-nine seconds was a fine pace. Sometimes I surprised myself and finished with a seven-and-a-half minute mile, but that was infrequent. To my mind, that made me "sort of" a runner, because many runners ran in a week what I ran in a month, and would view my efforts, perhaps not with disdain, but with at least some measure of condescension.

However, that track record came to an abrupt stop when I strained a muscle in my back so severely that I was all but immobile. It was probably a slipped disc. Whatever it was, it took me completely by surprise: I didn't expect my back to derail my running … I thought it might be my ankles, which, after repeated strains, have become, well, my Achilles heel, or my knees (which derailed many runners I know). It was not only surprising, but it was also profoundly discouraging. I was now grieving for what had seemed an ideal form of exercise. When I ran, I wasn't dependent on anyone else. In fact, I could fit it into my schedule pretty much whenever it worked best. I could do it when I was traveling, and it didn't require any special equipment except a good pair of running shoes and a watch with a timer (shorts and a top are useful too).

I went into mourning as I contemplated a future without running. I had lost something of immense value, and I didn't fully realize how valuable it was until I didn't have it anymore. I didn't feel as fit, and now it was getting harder to keep those pounds off without working up a good sweat three times a week.

And yet, bummed as I was, it didn't turn out to be quite the calamity I thought it was. In fact it turned out to be an opportunity (imposed, admittedly) to rethink the goals I had been setting for my health and exercise, and in the process I discovered how one-dimensional I had become in my exercising. With this one dimension removed, I was forced to look at other forms of exercise. Most of all, it turned me into the student of exercise that I had never been when I was a healthy runner. I learned about the importance of developing the core (that's the central part of our bodies and the key to our equilibrium) and the impact it has on running.

For the first time I saw the difference between aerobic exercise and resistance training (and the value of each), and for the first time, I actually enjoyed lifting weights. I looked differently at my diet. And I got some great advice. A good friend, an aficionado of workout rooms, walked me through the equipment and steered me to the most useful. For the first time, I went to a chiropractor, and not only got relief for my back, but advice on exercises that would strengthen the muscles around my spine … which, to my great relief, eventually allowed me to run again.

Leadership is much like exercise. Leadership is multi-dimensional, and yet, just as I was one-dimensional in my exercise before my back injury, many leaders are one-dimensional in their leadership—different for different leaders, but one-dimensional nonetheless. Just as I was comfortable running and had no intention of stepping inside a workout room, leaders tend to stick to an approach that feels most comfortable. But at some point, something happens to make that approach impossible, at least for a while. And just as I needed a framework to make sense of exercise, so leaders need a framework to make sense of great leadership.

The Solution to this Complexity: A Comprehensive Framework

Most leaders rely on two inputs to guide their leadership:

1. Intuition
2. Experience

And that's a problem. Given the complexity of the world we lead in, at some point intuition and experience will inevitably let us down. Our intuition will mislead us and our experience will be inadequate—however long we have been around.

To make sense of this extraordinary complexity, we need more than just intuition and experience. We need a comprehensive framework that pulls together all the different facets and dimensions of leadership into a coherent whole. That may not sound like much of a solution, but don't be fooled … it is. So why is a framework so important for understanding and exercising great leadership?

Framework is a construction term. Together with the foundation, it is the essence of any building. The framework determines both the appearance of the building in terms of size and shape. It determines its functionality, whether a residential home or a commercial building. It also determines the strength of the building: the stronger the frame, the more it can withstand.

Framing determines where you place the key functions of the building, like the bedrooms, the bathrooms, the kitchen, and all the common areas. Framing determines where everything unseen goes—the plumbing, the electrical circuitry, the heating and cooling systems, and so on.

You can pick the right supplier for everything you put into the house when the framework is clear. You'll pick one vendor for the tiles, perhaps a different one to lay them, another for the bathroom components, and another for the kitchen appliances. You most likely won't buy the kitchen appliances from the person who lays your tiles.

You can select the appropriate suppliers because you know how the house is framed—you know where the kitchen is, you know its dimensions, and you can determine which appliances fit where. You know the dimensions of the bedrooms, which tell you what kind of bedroom furniture will fit in each one.

The same logic should apply to leadership and leadership development. But in its current form, it doesn't. Leadership development today—whether it's leaders looking to develop themselves or those tasked within an organization to develop its leaders—is like someone going to a home show, where multiple vendors offer every conceivable element of home construction and home improvement—kitchen appliances, bathroom accessories, bedroom furniture, living room furniture, dining room furniture, and everything else that fills a house. As this individual walks past these booths, he's drawn into one after another—a particular bedroom set, a special fridge, and the latest washing machine technology. He orders them all ... before he has even framed the house.

We dismiss this approach as foolish and irrational, and rightly so. But when it comes to leadership, that's exactly what we do.

Like our hapless visitor to the home show, leaders fall under the spell of beguiling models and approaches—whether it's systems thinking, emotional intelligence, situational leadership, business process reengineering, or whatever else—without knowing where it fits into the overall leadership framework. They end up buying a fridge when they need a bed; they end up applying systems thinking, for example, when what they need is emotional intelligence.

In *The End of Leadership*, Barbara Kellerman aptly describes the state of confusion in both leadership and the leadership industry (those who teach leadership). The problem is that many of those teaching leadership are as confused as those they are teaching, or worse, they are unashamedly peddling their one perspective—presenting emotional intelligence, for example, as the cure to every leadership problem. They are like a bedroom furniture salesman selling you a bed, even though you need a fridge. Like every other resource and discipline in leadership, emotional intelligence is the right approach for some contexts, but not every context. Bedroom furniture is for the bedroom, not the kitchen.

Barbara Kellerman's focus is more on academia. But the problem is much broader. The business press doesn't help. Because of the constant pressure, especially for the online and weekly press, to deliver an endless supply of solutions to the challenges of leadership, they become equal contributors to the confusion around leadership and leadership development. They behave like a desperate sales clerk at a drug store, working her way backwards down the pain medication aisle, one eye darting over the shelves, and the other on the pale and sickly individual following her, haltingly, down the aisle. "This worked for me once …" as she throws a packet at him. "My mother swears by this one …" with another packet lobbed in his direction. "Someone famous told me this worked for them …" And the packets keep coming, bouncing off his chest and arms, landing unopened on the floor.

Such is the business press, throwing one solution after another, based on an interview, a success story, or a corporate failure, which ends up littering the aisles of its readership with unopened packages.

This is not to say that the solutions aren't useful. They are, but only in the right context. You don't use a laxative to cure a headache. But if you need a laxative, it's helpful to take one. You just need to know when it's appropriate, useful, and relevant. And for that, when it comes to leadership, you need a framework.

The Power of a Framework

So is a framework for leadership important? Absolutely! Not only important … it's essential. That may not sound like the kind of solution you were looking for, but we can tell you that it *works*.

What will it do for you? How will it help you? In multiple ways:

✓ It will help you make sense of the complexity of leadership. In understanding the complexity of leadership, you will understand how you, in your particular role, whatever the level of your leadership responsibility, can help transform healthcare delivery.

✓ It will bring all the different disciplines and facets of leadership together into a coherent whole. Leadership education has become extraordinarily fragmented, and it has become much harder to connect the dots between the different disciplines of leadership. With a solid framework, you'll be able to connect the dots.

✓ It will assist in understanding how these disciplines interact and connect with each other.

✓ It will help you understand organizations in a new way—not only the one you are in currently, but also any future organization you will be part of. And it will help you understand healthcare as a much larger system, and how your leadership plays an important part in its transformation.

✓ You'll find yourself better positioned to identify the critical skill sets you need for the particular challenges you face in your current leadership role.

✓ You will know what books to read and what resources to use—because you will understand the needs of your current leadership context.

✓ You will understand what is required for positions you are aspiring to.

✓ You will learn a framework that you can apply to any leadership context you operate in.

✓ You will be able to avoid the pitfalls that derail otherwise promising careers of great leadership.

So what is this Framework? Keep reading for the answer ...

Chapter 10

What Is Great Leadership?

U nderstanding what great leadership looks like is essential to exercising it. Essential to understanding great leadership is recognizing the existence of a framework that pulls together the different elements of leadership and then expresses them in a coherent manner. That framework is the subject of this chapter.

Einstein once said that everything should be as simple as possible ... and no simpler. We need to consider a framework that makes sense of all this complexity, which makes it as simple as possible, and no simpler than that. With that said, what does *that* look like?

Character and Competence

In the spirit of Einstein, in its simplest, purest form, all leadership can be defined in terms of two fundamental concepts:

1. Character—the personal qualities that make for great leadership
2. Competence—the leadership skills you need for the particular leadership role you are currently exercising

Everything that has to do with leadership has to do with one or the other or both of these two fundamental components. You need both, just as you need the two wings to fly an aircraft. Which do you think is more important—character or competence? Which is better—competence without character, or character without competence? At least with the competence, you get the job done. But then again, if you don't have the character, how will people trust you so that you can get the job done in an ethical manner? This is an age-old debate, going back at least as far as Socrates and the fifth century BC. As Greek democracy made leadership more accessible to more people, the question of what type of leadership was required for the success of a young democracy became a subject of intense debate.

If you think competence is more important, you're in the same camp as Socrates, who landed squarely on the side of competence. "Under all human conditions," he argued, "human beings are most willing to obey those whom they believe to be the best. Thus in sickness they most readily obey the doctor, on board ship the pilot, on the farm the farmer, whom they think to be most skilled in his business." It is much more likely, he argues, "that one who clearly knows best what ought to be done will most easily gain the obedience of the others." These comments, captured by Xenophon, clearly underscore the importance Socrates attached to competence in leadership.

As it turns out, Socrates never actually wrote anything. In fact, it was his followers, in particular Plato and Xenophon, who recorded what he said. However, neither of them agreed with him. Xenophon argued that leaders can be highly competent, but if competence is the only basis for their leadership, people will follow them, not because they want to but because they have to. For people to *want* to follow a leader, the leader needs the qualities of character, not just the skills of competence.

Xenophon identified thirteen key qualities of great leadership. These qualities had to do with character rather than competence and included things like temperance, justice, tactfulness, sympathy, courage, generosity, and so on[25].

---

25 Xenophon's 13 qualities were temperance, justice, sagacity, amiability, presence of mind, tactfulness, humanity, sympathy, helpfulness, courage, magnanimity, generosity, and considerateness … virtually all having more to do with character than competence.

Aristotle, a disciple of Plato, was much less complicated. He identified four qualities of great leadership:

1. Justice
2. Temperance
3. Prudence
4. Fortitude.

This debate has never subsided, and ever since the days of Socrates, Xenophon, and Aristotle, character and competence have lived in tension—and very starkly so during the last few decades. In the nineties, all the emphasis was on competence with little thought to character, leading to the many spectacular scandals of recent years, where issues of character derailed otherwise highly competent leaders.

But leaders can also fail for a lack of competence, especially in such a complex world where the exercise of leadership is more demanding than it's ever been. Ultimately, leaders fall either because they don't understand the mechanics of leadership in all its complexity (a competence issue) or they break trust with those they lead and the community they serve (a character issue).

If competence gets you to the table, it's character that keeps you there. Jeffrey Pfeffer (from Stanford University) argues that the reason we have seen so much corruption surface in recent years may be that the business schools gave these highly competent and gifted leaders the technical tools without giving them the moral compass to use them. They got to the table because they used the tools well, but they were dismissed because they failed to use them appropriately.

So what's the difference? Character is about choices, and competence is about skill. Character is about how we choose to use the acquired competence.

So which is more important: character or competence? You would be right if you concluded that both are equally important.

The essence of great leadership—and the solution to the tension between character and competence—is the simple act of giving due importance to both.

Defining Character in Leadership

As you read about character in leadership, ask yourself these questions:

- What does character in leadership look like in my particular role—as a physician, a legislator, a regulator, a hospital administrator, an insurance provider, a manufacturer for the healthcare industry—or as any other stakeholder role I may fulfill in healthcare?
- What does it mean for my immediate sphere of influence?
- Is the pursuit of character in my sphere of influence at odds with the pursuit of character for healthcare in general?

And with these questions in mind, what do we mean by character in leadership?

Character in leadership is about pursuing noble ends through noble means. This definition has two components, and here again, you need both. It's not enough to pursue noble ends; it's also important to pursue them with noble means. It's not just what you pursue, but how you actually pursue them.

What do we mean by noble ends? Noble means is anything that is characterized by focusing on others, by adding value, and by representing something larger than you or your organization. That spreads a wide net. In fact, a noble end is anything that doesn't harm the supplier or the user. For example, people in construction, the food industry, and of course healthcare are all perceived to pursue a noble end.

So, in a nutshell, noble means is about pursuing these ends with integrity, courage, self-sacrifice, and humility.

‖‖

A Study in Contrasts

Consider John Adams and Thomas Jefferson in the light of this definition of character. If you've read David McCullough's biography of John Adams, you will know that Jefferson doesn't come out looking good, despite being the icon that he is in American history. John Adams, on the other hand, comes out as the unsung hero of the American Revolution. The reason is very simple: they both pursued the same noble end (independence from Britain), but only one, John Adams, pursued it with noble means.

John Adams was a man of tremendous integrity. He was the only lawyer willing to defend some British soldiers accused of massacring a group of colonials. It was an immensely unpopular undertaking, because the colonists were ready to lynch them without a trial, but he did it because they deserved a just trial, and he displayed the courage to do what he considered right. And in the end, he won their acquittal. In addition:

- He endured long separations from his wife Abigail, at one time for five straight years (some would consider that a blessing; for Adams, it was a hardship).
- He bore the brunt of slander and misunderstanding.
- He sacrificed financially.
- He agonized over the birth of the new republic.
- He expended tremendous energy and effort to win others over to the cause of independence. He traveled over 29,000 miles for the cause of independence—far more than any of his contemporaries. His reputation in England was such that, had the fight for independence proved vain, he was singled out for hanging without consideration for pardon.

Jefferson made no such sacrifices. He pursued the same end, but not with the same noble means.

|||||||||||||||||||||||||||||||||||||||||||||||||||||||||||||||||||||||||||||||||||||||||||||||||||||||||||||||||||||||||||||||||||||

Character in leadership is important for two reasons, as outlined by Os Guinness[26], a seasoned observer and commentator on American society for the past thirty years. He states:

---

26 Os Guinness, *Character Counts*

"Far from a cliché or a matter of hollow civic piety, character in leaders is important for two key reasons:

Externally, character provides the point of trust that links leaders with followers.

Internally, character is the part-gyroscope, part-brake that provides the leader's strongest source of bearings and restraint. In many instances the first prompting to do good and the last barrier against doing wrong are the same—character."

According to Guinness's comment, character is critical externally because:

1. It builds trust.
2. It helps us make better choices.

Defining Competence in Leadership

As you read through the following description of competence in leadership, ask yourself these questions:

- What does competence in leadership look like in my particular role— as a physician, a legislator, a regulator, a hospital administrator, a manufacturer for the healthcare industry?
- What does it mean for my immediate sphere of influence?
- Is the pursuit of competence in my sphere of influence at odds with the pursuit of competence for healthcare in general?

How do we define competence in leadership? Competence in leadership is created through an understanding of the right kind of leadership, applied appropriately to our particular leadership context, as we pursue our noble ends.

This is where much of the confusion lies, and we can dispel that confusion by thinking of competence in leadership in terms of three dimensions:

1. The entire organization needs to be led.
2. The tasks and operations within the organization need to be led.
3. And the people within the organization need to be led.

Each one has a very different skill set, and much of the confusion around leadership comes from the confusion around these three dimensions.

Think of it like a ship. For a ship to run well, it needs three kinds of leadership:

1. Organizational Leadership
2. Operational Leadership
3. People Leadership

First of all, the ship as a whole needs to be led. That means it needs a captain on the bridge whose focus is external, and who determines the destination, making sure it doesn't hit another ship, doesn't hit an iceberg, doesn't run aground, and most important, doesn't miss its port of destination.

But this first kind of leadership is useless without the second—the one that leads all the tasks and operations within the ship. All the functionally critical tasks within the ship need to be led—the cooks feeding the crew, the engineers maintaining the engines, and everyone else fulfilling the multitude of tasks essential for the ship to function well—all these tasks need to be efficiently led and executed. These leaders need to know where the ship is going, and what its external conditions are. But their leadership focus is internal. And it's vital: it doesn't matter how good the captain is at avoiding collisions and reaching the right destination, because if that ship is dead in the water—it's still not going anywhere.

And finally, the people on the ship need to be led. They need to be in roles for which they are qualified and suited, the expectations of their performance need to be clear, and the development and support necessary for their effectiveness need to be provided.

We call the first *Organizational Leadership* (the captain on the bridge), the second *Operational Leadership* (the tasks within the ship), and the third *People Leadership* (all the people working on the ship). In other words:

- *Organizational Leadership* is externally focused. Its concern is where the organization as a whole is heading, what conditions it currently faces, and what conditions it is likely to face.
- *Operational Leadership* is internally focused. Its concern is how it functions internally, making sure that all the tasks and operations it needs to perform are well-led and well-accomplished.
- *People Leadership* is about bringing out the best in the people within the organization, whatever their level and whatever their role may be.

Each one of these three dimensions has a critical skill set and key set of functions.

This is not about technical or functional competence or expertise. You may have an extraordinary level of competence in a particular branch of medicine, or in some aspect of running a medical institution, like finance, marketing, project management, or something else. That's not what we mean here. This is about competence in these three key dimensions of leadership: Organizational Leadership, Operational Leadership, and People Leadership. The more present they are, the better led the organization. And in the image of the diagram below the more they overlap, the better-led the organization.

The Competence Side of Great Leadership

The Three Dimensions of Leadership

Organizational Leadership

A Well-Led Organization

Operational Leadership

People Leadership

© 2006 LeaderDevelopment Inc.

The Interplay Between Character and Competence

A ship can run perfectly, with every dimension of leadership fully exercised, but if its cargo is contraband, drugs, or human traffic, it doesn't matter how well-run it is, because its existence is a bane.

So both character and competence are indispensable, and both are equally important. But what does that look like? What does it look like when you have both? Or when you have neither? Or when you have one without the other?

In the diagram below, the vertical axis on the left is character, identified as high and low, and the horizontal access on the bottom is competence, again identified as high and low.

Character & Competence in Leadership

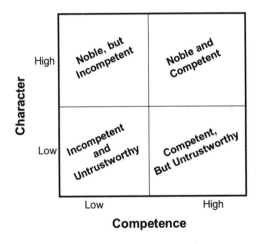

© 2012 Bell/Shoultz

The top right quadrant is the Holy Grail, where character and competence combine to give us noble and competent leadership. This is where the truly great leaders camp out—George Washington, John Adams, Abraham Lincoln, Winston Churchill, Mother Teresa, Nelson Mandela, and the many others, known and unknown, inside and outside the marketplace. These are the people to emulate, and this is the quadrant in which we strive to climb. Rest assured that it is far from unattainable.

The bottom left quadrant is a different story. It is the diametric opposite, and the one to avoid. It is surprising how many leaders survive in this quadrant—and how long they survive. This is where a leader acts as a tyrant—overpoweringly intimidating and destructively incompetent. It's the absolute antithesis of great leadership. You may have worked for someone who was incompetent but by sheer bullying managed to hold onto and extend his or her power. You most likely didn't stay for long.

The bottom right quadrant is a hybrid: high competence, low character. This is someone who provides excellent leadership in terms of the three dimensions we discussed earlier. However, you just don't trust what they do or say. You admire and respect their talent, but you're guarded. Sometimes leaders from the bottom left quadrant improve their level of competence and move into the bottom right hand quadrant. Their character hasn't changed; they've simply become more competent. These leaders can be even more destructive than those in the bottom left quadrant—precisely because they are competent. The bottom right quadrant is not a pretty one.

The top left quadrant—high character, low competence—reflects noble but inept leadership. This would be someone you like and appreciate. You trust them for their character, but not for their competence. Because they're not exercising their leadership with the kind of competence their role requires, however much you like them as a person, you end up frustrated because you're not getting the leadership you need.

As we consider these four quadrants, they beg an important question: how easy is it move from one quadrant to another? Generally, it is easier to move horizontally than vertically—from low competence to high competence, because we just need to know how to apply the right mix of Organizational, Operational, and People Leadership to our particular role. It is also, unfortunately, easier to move downwards on the vertical scale—from high character to low character. We see it in young leaders, who start out altruistically, but with the pressure to produce results end up making compromises that eventually compromise their character. Correspondingly, it is much harder to move up the vertical scale—from low character to high character. Rarely does a leader move from the bottom right-hand quadrant into the upper right-hand quadrant. It happens, but it takes an epiphany of epic proportions. More likely, they self-destruct, but that may take longer than we expect, and in the meantime, their leadership remains very destructive.

As you consider these four quadrants, think about how you'd categorize certain leaders. For example, where would you put the past presidents of the United States? Where would you put Nixon, Carter, Reagan, Clinton, the two Bushes, and Obama? Where would you put some of the prominent global leaders of the modern times? Where would you put Mandela, Gandhi, Hitler, Stalin, Mao Tse Tung, bin Laden, Churchill, Thatcher, or anyone else that comes to mind? Where would you put some of the prominent business leaders of the past decades? Where would you put the various bosses you have worked for?

Most importantly, where would you put yourself? How would you describe the overall tone of leadership within your organization? In other words, which quadrant would you put it in? Plenty of important questions to consider.

So there you have the interplay between character and competence. You need both. One without the other is not great leadership, and one without the other carries its own particular dangers. As Samuel Johnson put it, "Integrity [character] without knowledge [competence] is weak and useless, and knowledge [competence] without integrity [character] is dangerous and dreadful."

Over the next few chapters we will address both competence and character in greater detail. We start with competence. As you read through these chapters, consider the following questions:

- *How would you say the absence of either has contributed to the difficulties we currently face in healthcare?*
- *Where do you see character and competence exercised effectively in healthcare?*
- *Which elements of each resonate with you particularly for the specific leadership challenges you face?*

Develop competence, and you have skilled leadership. Add character, and you have great leadership. Our goal is to help you build both, so that you can exercise truly great leadership.

Chapter 11

What is Competence in Leadership?

I f leadership seems hard, complex and confusing, that's because it is! The purpose of this book is to help you as a leader—whatever your role as a stakeholder in healthcare—successfully deal with that complexity and decisively dispel that confusion. Our goal is to lift the fog so that you can see what kind of leadership you need to exercise.

Much of that confusion comes from the confusion around what we mean by *competence* in leadership. In this chapter, our intent is to dispel that confusion by laying out the principles of competence in leadership. In the next chapter, we will apply them directly to healthcare.

First of all, we need to be clear about what is not considered competence in leadership. We have said this before, but it bears repeating: it is not technical or functional competence. You may be an outstanding doctor, nurse, technician, engineer, accountant, marketer, or business analyst—but that's technical or functional competence, and very different from what we mean by competence in leadership. You can have these skills and still not be a great leader.

Nor is competence in leadership the mastery of one particular expression of leadership. Developing a clear sense of direction for the organization is a critical element of competence in leadership, but it is one among several. Systems thinking is also important, but again, it is only one element of competence in leadership. Emotional intelligence is also useful, but again, it isn't the only one.

Theologian Francis Schaeffer once compared truth to a table. Truth, he argued, is a table—a pretty big one, with conflicting theological positions on opposite sides. Our tendency is to pick a point on the table and call it truth, when in fact the whole table is the truth. He wasn't arguing for the relativity of truth, because the table does have an edge ... at some point you can fall off the table, and you're no longer dealing with truth. His point was that truth is much bigger than we think it is.

Schaeffer's illustration could just as easily be applied to competence in leadership. People stake a claim on one point of the table and define leadership in terms of that one point—whether it's vision casting, systems thinking, emotional intelligence or anything else they might grab onto—when in fact they've picked only one point on the table. They forget or ignore the fact that there are plenty of other points on the table, with plenty of people grabbing hold of each one. In fact the table is pretty crowded. And very noisy! With all this noise and confusion, how do we make sense of it all?

The best way to bring clarity to such a crowded table is to take a step back and make sense of the whole table. We need to take a bird's eye view. And when we do, we see three very distinct dimensions to competence in leadership (as we discussed in the previous chapter):

- *Organizational Leadership*, which is about leading the **entire organization**
- *Operational Leadership*, which is about leading the **tasks and operations** within the organization
- *People Leadership*, which is about leading the **people** within the organization

Think of the ship we described in the last chapter. A well-run ship needs all three: a captain on the bridge steering the whole ship (Organizational

Leadership), engineers keeping the ship running, cooks providing meals, and maintenance staff maintaining the ship (Operational Leadership), and everyone in any kind of leadership role making sure that the right people are in the right roles, giving them the support, training, and resources they need (People Leadership).

Competence in Leadership:
The Three Dimensions

Organizational Leadership

Operational Leadership

A Well-Led Organization

People Leadership

Each of these dimensions has a very different skill set, and once we understand what these different skill sets look like, we will have gone a long way to dispel the confusion around competence in leadership. And that is our intent in this chapter and the next. In this chapter we will explain these different skill sets, and in the next we will apply them directly to healthcare.

As you read through this chapter, keep in mind that these principles apply both to the leadership it takes to lead a healthcare organization (a hospital or government agency, for example), as well as to the leadership it takes to shape healthcare as a sector.

It will help to address these three dimensions from an organizational perspective and from an individual perspective. We need to see how important these three dimensions are for the whole organization, and we also need to see how they apply to your own particular individual context. So first, the organizational perspective.

Competence in Leadership for the Organization

The Key Functions of Organizational Leadership

"Enterprise without a leader," argues author Patrick Henlon, "is like a headless elephant. It may eventually get somewhere, but only by destroying everything in its path along the way."[27] Henlon is describing the absence of Organizational Leadership, and its absence does indeed exercise a powerfully destructive force. Its presence, however, is equally powerful—for good, especially when it fulfills its three main functions well:

- *Creating* a clear sense of direction for the organization, constantly clarifying it.
- *Aligning* the organization and its resources to that direction.
- *Selling* the entire organization on that direction, so that all embrace it and buy into it.

You'll notice that it creates an acronym: Organizational Leadership is "CAS" leadership.

C ... Create and Clarify Direction
A ... Align the Organization and its Resources
S ... Sell the Message of the Direction

At first blush, you'd think that this applies only to the CEO of the organization and his or her leadership team. It is true that those functions are particularly important for people at the top of an organization: they need to make sure that everyone knows where this ship is going, that it's setting the best course to get there, and that it's taking into account every relevant piece of external information—storms, currents, other ships, and so on.

---

27 Patrick Henlon, *Primal Branding*

But if you are not leading the whole organization, but rather a piece of it, it's still just as crucial for you. The reason why is that you and your people interface with other people and departments outside of your own. If you are running an accounting department or an IT department, or departments of emergency care, pharmacy, nursing, medicine and surgery, you still have an external context to your unit or department, and that external context is the rest of the organization. Whatever the department or unit you lead, you have an Organizational Leadership responsibility to consider how your department best serves the rest of the organization.

So with that in mind, what does it mean *to create and clarify direction*?

To set a clear direction, you need to pay attention to three important drivers:

- *A clear sense of purpose or mission* (we use the words interchangeably). What is the purpose you are fulfilling? What is your mission? If you are leading the entire organization, the entire organization needs a clear purpose. If you are leading an IT department, an ICU unit or an accounting department, your department or unit needs one. Remember, how you define its purpose will shape its performance. You may think that an IT department's purpose is pretty obvious, but you would be surprised by how many ways it could be defined—and the way you, as the leader of IT, define the mission and purpose of IT will shape the behavior of the people who work in it.

- *A clear vision for the future.* At an organizational level, the senior leadership needs to have and to communicate a clear sense of where the organization is going. But so does every business unit leader and every department leader. If you are leading an accounting department or an IT department, what do you see it accomplishing two years or five years from now? What will it look like? How will it be contributing? How will it be performing better than it is now?

- *A clear set of values.* Values define how your people behave when they are fulfilling the mission and dealing with people outside your department. The organization as a whole needs clear values, and so does the unit you are leading.

Everyone in the organization needs to be exercising Organizational Leadership appropriately for his or her particular level of leadership responsibility. But this is particularly important for the leaders at the top of the organization. If they are not giving clear direction for the whole organization, they make it much harder for everyone else they lead to relate what they are doing to the organization's bigger picture. If, on the other hand, the leaders at the top of the organization are giving a clear sense of direction, there is a much greater likelihood of everyone else aligning their efforts to that direction.

What does it mean to *align the organization and its resources*?

- To align well, you need to ensure that all the systems and processes within the organization or within your department are reinforcing your organization's purpose, vision, and values. It means paying attention to anything that might be hindering their pursuit. It means making sure you select people who are in tune with the direction you have set. It means making sure that whatever form training and development takes, it reinforces everything that you have defined as important, whether as the organization or as a department. Alignment isn't easy, but it's vital.

What does it mean to *sell the direction to the organization*?

- Selling the direction is about creating buy-in. More than just knowing your purpose, vision, and values, you want people to embrace and own it. You want it to be theirs as much as yours. That takes effort and intentionality, but when you generate that kind of ownership, you release an energy you never suspected existed.

So that's Organizational Leadership—CAS leadership. It's a challenge to exercise it well, but it is a lot easier to do so if we understand its importance. When leaders *don't* understand its importance, what does the organization look like? What happens to an organization when Organizational Leadership is weak or absent (as in the diagram below)?

Dysfunctional
Organizational Leadership

You would probably describe it as rudderless ... without clear direction ... with its people at cross-purposes ... operating in silos ... in a highly charged political environment ... and internally competitive, as people pursue their own agendas instead of a widely embraced corporate and organizational purpose.

Sounds pretty dysfunctional and unhealthy, right? But that's what an organization looks like when Organizational Leadership is weak.

Before we leave Organizational Leadership, a quick observation. While it is true that every level of leadership within an organization has a measure of Organizational Leadership, it is also true that its importance increases as leadership responsibilities increase. As a rule of thumb, the closer you are to frontline management in your leadership role, the more your primary function will be Operational Leadership, and the closer you are to top management in your leadership role, the more your primary function will be Organizational Leadership. But that doesn't mean that if you are closer to the operations, you can ignore Organizational Leadership ... you can't!

And now to Operational Leadership.

The Key Functions of Operational Leadership
If Organizational Leadership is about guiding and steering the whole ship, Operational Leadership is about keeping it running. Without this internally focused leadership, the ship is dead in the water.

Exercising great Operational Leadership requires doing three things well:

- *Planning and shaping* the processes within the organization.
- *Organizing* people and resources around those processes.
- *Measuring* the performance of those processes and solving whatever problems arise.

Again, it creates an acronym: Operational Leadership is "POM" leadership.

P ... *Plan and Shape the Processes*
O ... *Organize the People and Processes*
M ... *Measure and Problem Solve*

Systems thinking is at the heart of Operational Leadership. If your leadership role is predominantly operational, you need to become comfortable with systems thinking. You need to see your operational environment as a system, subject to all the internal and external processes that shape and mold it. Great Operational Leadership means understanding those systems and shaping them to provide the best delivery of the service you provide.

Systems are everywhere. They are part of life. Our bodies are made up of different systems: the nervous system, the intestinal system, the skeletal system, and so on. They all interact with each other. Whenever we travel, we're at the mercy of changing weather systems, which may disrupt the air traffic system—and depending on the schedule we have to keep, it may do a number on our nervous system!

What happens when Operational Leadership is weak or missing (as in the diagram below)?

Dysfunctional
Operational Leadership

You might point to obvious inefficiencies … or to the widespread duplication of effort and resources … or to the high level of frustration throughout the organization. And if you probed a little deeper, you would uncover a host of unintended consequences because in the confusion of inefficiency, people are not making the connection between a decision and its reverberations throughout the organization.

Pretty dysfunctional, right? And so is People Leadership when it isn't exercised. Let's look at that one.

The Key Functions of People Leadership
To exercise great People Leadership, you need to:

- ***Select and match*** people well—pick the right ones and match their strengths to the opportunities that need those strengths.
- ***Explain and Clarify*** your expectations, not just in what the people they lead should do, but also in how well they do it.
- ***Motivate and Develop*** your people.

Again, it creates an acronym: People Leadership is "SEM" leadership.

S ... Select and Match
E ... Explain and Clarify
M ... Motivate and Develop

This is not about your ability to relate well with people, important though that is.[28] This is about bringing out the best in the people you lead. It's not about your relationship with them; it's about their performance. It's about elevating talent, which requires the three skills we just identified—the "SEM" skills.

When People Leadership is absent, what does that look like in an organization (as in the diagram below)?

Dysfunctional **People Leadership**

High turnover is likely. The research is pretty conclusive that people quit bosses, not organizations. And they quit their bosses because these bosses aren't focused on putting people in the right fit, aren't setting clear expectations, aren't motivating them, aren't creating motivating environments, and aren't intentionally developing them. No wonder they leave! And those who stay are most likely unhappy and disgruntled, and would leave if they could!

---

28   Relating well to people and developing people skills is more related to the Pyramid of Personal Qualities, which we will be discussing in the chapters on character in leadership.

This, too, is important to get right. And notice how these three dimensions play off each other. If the leaders who should provide good Organizational Leadership actually do so, they make it much easier for those in Operational Leadership roles to provide the kind of leadership they should be exercising. Likewise, if both Organizational Leadership and Operational Leadership are being well exercised, it makes it much easier for leaders at every level to deliver good People Leadership.

Competence in Leadership for the Individual

That's enough for now on applying these three dimensions of leadership to the organization as a whole (the organizational perspective). What about the individual perspective? What do these dimensions look like for an individual, whatever their level of leadership responsibility?

Most importantly, how do these three dimensions apply to you and *your* particular leadership role?

That's where the Leadership Cube™ will help you. But before we introduce the Leadership Cube™, we need to address a particularly thorny and tense relationship between two dimensions in particular.

The Relationship between Organizational Leadership and Operational Leadership

This has always been a tense relationship. The tension comes from the fact that over the career of a leader, the mix of these two changes. This means that as a leader takes on more responsibility, the leadership skill set needed becomes *less* of one and *more* of the other.

In the diagram below, the horizontal axis at the bottom represents the amount of time a leader spends in each one—in Organizational Leadership and Operational Leadership. Notice that there is a big difference between the CEO/President (at the top) and the Assistant Project Manager (at the bottom)—the CEO spends most of his or her time in Organizational Leadership, and the Assistant Project Manager spends most of his or her time in Operational Leadership.

The diagonal line reflects how the relationship changes with each new promotion (in practice, the diagonal line is not a perfectly straight line, and the point at which leaders make a shift from a more Operational Leadership focus to a more Organizational Leadership focus depends to a large extent on the organization).

If we applied this to a healthcare organization, the titles on the left would most likely be:

- CEO/President
- Vice President
- Chair of Major Committee
- Chair of Department
- Chair of Division
- Chair of a Section
- Project Manager
- Assistant Project Manager

The diagram above, of course, describes an ideal world, where leaders understand and appreciate the changing nature of their roles and adjust accordingly. The problem is that very few leaders actually do understand the shifts they need to make as they progress through these different roles. Like most leaders, they typically start their careers applying a much more operational focus in their leadership … and they never stop applying it! They don't understand the changing requirements of each new role. They keep doing what they did before, even though their responsibilities require them to think and act differently—thinking beyond the confines of their operations to the broader context outside their organization or unit. They are like the captain of the ship who keeps coming down to oversee the engine room, leaving the bridge unattended, with the undeniable accusation of micromanagement, the inevitable loss of organizational focus, and the rising frustration within the organization.

Here's what it looks like … not a pretty picture!

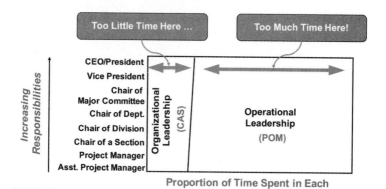

© Antony Bell 2015

This happens all too frequently. Why? Well, why do people get promoted? Because they are good at what they do. And when they get promoted, what do they do? They keep doing what they were good at before they got promoted, without realizing that the recipe for success at one level can become the recipe for failure at the next. The inevitable response is to work harder, which is no solution.

Now that we are familiar with the face of the Cube—let's look at it in its entirety.

How Does People Leadership Fit In?

As a reminder, the face of the Cube reflects different levels of leadership, as illustrated below, with senior-level leadership at the top of the face and front-line leadership at the bottom.

Applying the Right Leadership Mix At Each Level of Leadership

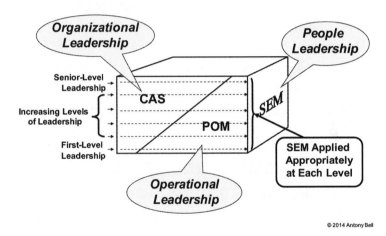

© 2014 Antony Bell

It is People Leadership that makes it a cube, because People Leadership (the "SEM" functions) reinforces the relationship between Organizational Leadership and Operational Leadership—at every level on the face of the Cube.

If People Leadership is essential to the full expression of a healthy relationship between Organizational Leadership and Operational Leadership, how do the SEM functions actually apply to each level? Good question! Take the CEO of the organization. Is he or she expected to apply SEM to his or her role? Absolutely! What about a frontline leader—is he or she expected to apply SEM to his or her role? Absolutely! And so is everyone else in between. But will they apply it in the same way? No. Consider the differences in the roles between a CEO and an assistant project manager:

- Their *skill sets* are different. It takes a very different set of skills to lead an organization than those you need to lead a team on the front lines of the organization.
- Their *scope* is different. For the front line leader, it's his or her team or crew; for the CEO it's the entire organization—and beyond.
- Their *timeframes* are different. The frontline leader's timeframe is measured in hours, days, or perhaps weeks. For the CEO, it's measured in years.

But despite these differences, both need to apply the principles of SEM. They will apply them differently because they are applying them at different levels of the organization—but they will both apply them nonetheless.

What happens when People Leadership is weak? That's the cube on the right in the diagram below, which really isn't a cube at all! It's a thin, wobbly slice, which tells us that when People Leadership is weak, the whole cube is weak. In

Strong and Weak
People Leadership (SEM)

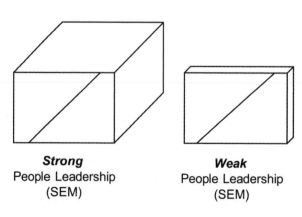

Strong
People Leadership
(SEM)

Weak
People Leadership
(SEM)

fact, it can easily topple or be toppled without the stability that comes from the skill sets associated with People Leadership. By contrast, the cube on the left is a pretty solid cube, because People Leadership is strong. That one is not going to topple over. Such is the organization where People Leadership is appropriately and intentionally exercised at every level of leadership.

||||||||||||||||||||||||||||||||||||||||||||||||||||||||||||||||||||||||||||||||||||||||||||||||||||||||||||||||||||||||||||||||

The US Army and the Leadership Cube (Antony)

A few years ago, I participated in a panel organized by the US Army to discuss what leadership development in the Army will look 15 to 20 years from now. The Army had been doing some innovative thinking, and they brought together a group of academics and business people to help them with that thinking.

Applying the Right Mix at Each Leadership Level

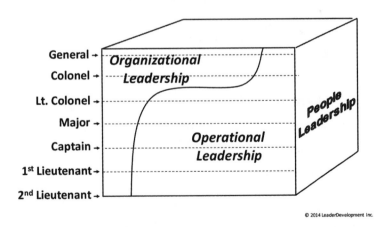

© 2014 LeaderDevelopment Inc.

The application of the Leadership Cube™ was actually very relevant to their context, and it mirrors much of what is going on outside the military in the marketplace.

In the past, the nature of military leadership changed significantly around the level of Colonel, and at that point it typically became more strategic and less tactical—it transitioned from a more Operational Leadership focus to a more Organizational Leadership focus. And for many, just as in the corporate world, that was a difficult transition.

Desert Storm changed that transition, and the war in Afghanistan reinforced that change. From that point on, strategic decisions that in the past were made by Colonels were now being made by Captains. It was the Captains who were making critical strategic decisions, and it was the Captains who were fulfilling the negotiating and diplomatic functions with local militia and local officials that in the past had been the responsibility of the Colonels. In effect, the line shifted—downwards.

Applying the Right Mix at Each Leadership Level

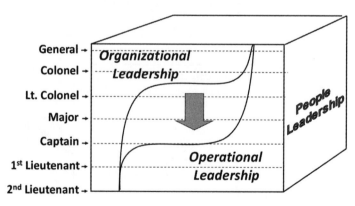

© 2014 LeaderDevelopment Inc.

This example tells us a couple of things. It reminds us that the diagonal line is not really a straight line—that there's typically a level at which it changes significantly.

It also shows us the importance of getting the face of the Cube right so that People Leadership can be genuinely effective. If the Army didn't change and kept training Captains without recognizing the shift in their roles—in other words kept training them as if the real shift still took place at the level of Colonel—what would be the result? You would have Captains ill-equipped and ill-prepared for the responsibilities their new roles demanded.

||||||||||||||||||||||||||||||||||||||||||||||||||||||||||||||||||||||||||||||||||||||||||||||||||||||||||||||||||||||||||||||||||||||||||||

Why Is Competence in Leadership so Important in Healthcare?

In this chapter, our goal was to lay out a framework for competence in leadership. In the next chapter, we will apply it directly to healthcare. And we will see that competence in leadership is vital, because it addresses so much that is critical to solving the issues of healthcare. And competence in leadership underscores why it's so important to focus on the ultimate vision of relentlessly pursuing the best care for patients, achieving the best outcomes, ensuring the highest level of safety, and creating the best possible service … all the while controling costs by eliminating waste and redundant care.

To do so requires organizational leaders who establish the vison, who align the organization to support those who will accomplish the vision, and who sell the vision so that everyone in the organization owns it. It requires operational leaders capable of understanding and shaping the systems, both within their immediate sphere as well as in the broader context of healthcare. And it requires leaders who know how to bring out the best in the people they lead.

What does that actually look like in healthcare?

How do we take the principles outlined in this chapter and apply them to healthcare?

That is the focus of the next chapter.

Chapter 12

How Will Competence in Leadership Transform Healthcare?

I f you have had any doubts that great leadership can transform healthcare, we hope that they have been dispelled. But the question remains: *how* will it transform healthcare? And more specifically, how will the kind of *competence* in leadership that we described in the previous chapter transform healthcare?

Healthcare delivery is an extraordinarily complex system, but that doesn't make it impermeable to great leadership. It is amazing the impact great leadership can have on an organization, a movement, or even a whole sector like healthcare. The key is that the right leaders step up to the leadership challenge required by healthcare. For great leadership to permeate healthcare, it needs to be harnessed by two critically important groups whose expressions of great leadership look very different:

- The healthcare providers who actually practice medicine and provide the delivery.
- The supporting stakeholders who make that delivery either harder or easier—policy makers, regulators, payers, medical equipment manufacturers, pharmaceutical companies, and service providers in healthcare-related fields (legal, technical, financial, HR, etc.).

In this chapter we explore the relationship between the two and what competence in leadership looks like in each case.

The Need for Providers to Embrace their Leadership Role

If anyone is in a critical place to lead, it is healthcare providers like doctors, nurses, nurse practitioners, pharmacists, leaders of medical organizations, medical administrators, project managers, system engineers, and financial officers.

Their leadership is vital, as no one else is in the position to have the kind of impact they can have. They stand in a pivotal place. No one else can provide the particular kind of leadership that only they can provide. Other stakeholders are vitally important too, but if the other stakeholders do all they can and should, and providers don't exercise the kind of leadership they can and should exercise, then the transformation of healthcare delivery will go nowhere. The importance of their role is unequivocal.

But they must embrace this role by accepting the responsibility and welcome the accountability that comes with pursuing the right style of medical practice, delivering the right kinds of outcomes, and providing the right kind of service with the right level of safety. They need to take ownership for the appropriateness of what is done to and for patients—because much of it is in their hands.

Just how pivotal is their role? In simple terms, total spending in healthcare has two components: the price paid for each service and the rate of use for those services. On the price side, providers share the responsibility for this parameter with patients, insurers, employers, and government. On the use rate side, providers clearly have a central role to play in the overall spending to the extent they control the rate of use of services.

It is time for providers to step up and embrace this responsibility and become accountable. And by doing so, they will earn the respect and authority that comes with great leadership, and thereby restore the practice of medicine to the place of eminence it once held in the past.

Admittedly, that is no easy challenge. Leadership in healthcare is hard. Abundant confusion persists today about who should lead and how. Healthcare generally is confused about who has the primary responsibility to lead and who should lead through supporting roles. Fortunately, all that confusion can be dispelled with a clear vision for patient-centered, high-value healthcare. With such a vision, these roles become clear. Which brings us to the importance of the relationship between providers and other stakeholders.

The Relationship between Providers and Stakeholders

The relationship between the two groups is critical. In fact, if we were forced to reduce the problem of healthcare to one single phenomenon, it would be this: the *providers of healthcare* don't understand how to exercise great leadership, and *those who support them* don't know how to exercise the leadership to support them.

The Current Delivery of Healthcare

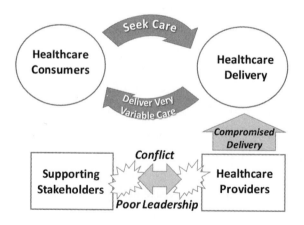

The relationship between healthcare providers and their supporting stakeholders is fraught with tension and looks something like the diagram above—with the consequences for healthcare consumers that the diagram suggests. That is, consumers receiving fragmented and unpredictable care, finding access difficult, experiencing widely variable outcomes, feeling unsure of adequate and uniform safety, and landed with the soaring, inexplicable, and burdensome costs of care.

Instead of this built-in conflict and tension, what do we *want* healthcare delivery to look like? What *could* it look like? What *should* it look like?

It could and should look something like the diagram below.

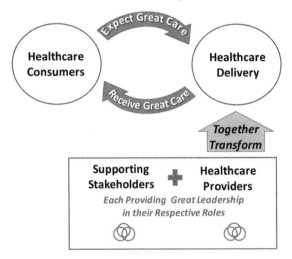

The Desired Delivery of Healthcare

In such a state, healthcare providers and the supporting stakeholders all understand the leadership roles needed and supposed to be exercised. Instead of competing, they complement and collaborate. Each party, according to their respective roles, exercises the right kind of Organizational Leadership, Operational Leadership, and People Leadership.

So what does it look like in the case of the providers and for the supporting stakeholders? Let's start with the bigger picture, discussing the roles played by the supporting stakeholders.

The Role of Stakeholders

Stakeholders are those who contribute to healthcare delivery without actually delivering it. Such stakeholders include:

1. Policy Makers and Regulators
   - Policy makers at the federal level (Congress)

- Policy makers at the state level (state legislatures)
- Public administrators at federal and state levels (federal and state government)
- Regulators at federal and state levels (federal and state government)

2. Payers
   - Insurance companies
   - Employers
   - The federal and state governments as buyers of healthcare delivery

3. Manufacturers and Service Providers
   - Equipment manufacturers
   - Pharmaceutical, biotech, and IT companies
   - Specialized Service Providers (legal, medical, technological, financial, etc.)

All three of these categories are important. Without equipment manufacturers and drug companies, for example, physicians could not provide the care they do. But the most critical supporting stakeholders are policy makers and regulators. They dictate the direction, and they provide the incentives. If they provide the right incentives, the other supporting stakeholders will follow the incentives. They create either a functional environment or a dysfunctional environment. The regulations they issue directly impact what goes on inside each domain within the healthcare delivery system, as well as the interactions among the domains. They shape not only the domains, but also how they interface.

So what does competence in leadership look like for policy makers and regulators? How do Organizational Leadership, Operational Leadership, and People Leadership express themselves in their particular roles?

No One on the Bridge

In Chapters 10 and 11, we compared competence in leadership to a ship. The captain on the bridge provides the Organizational Leadership, those who make the ship run efficiently provide the Operational Leadership, and all the leaders at every level within the ship provide People Leadership—bringing out the best in the people working for them.

Confusion around these three roles is the greatest source of leadership dysfunction. When the Captain is absent from the bridge, the ship is at great risk. It's going full steam because it runs well, but there is no leadership on the bridge to give it direction. It won't be long before it hits another ship or an iceberg or runs aground, and it certainly would not be able to find its port of destination. In fact, from an Operational Leadership perspective, the better run the ship is, the more dangerous it is if there is no one on the bridge to direct that power and energy.

The focus of policy makers is on the direction of healthcare as a whole. Their place is on the bridge, focusing firmly on Organizational Leadership. Their job is to make sure that the ship can handle the weather conditions ahead, that it doesn't run aground, that it doesn't collide with another ship ... and most important, that it reaches its port of destination.

Unfortunately, those who should be setting the direction for healthcare can't agree on the direction. There are too many captains steering the ship. When it comes to healthcare, policy makers are like a ship leaving New York harbor and two miles out to sea, the captain summons his senior officers, and asks, "OK, where shall we go? Liverpool? Lisbon?

Policy Makers
and the Leadership Cube™

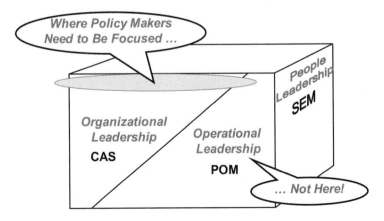

© 2015 Antony Bell

Buenos Aires? Cape Town?" An impossibility on a ship, and a sad reality in healthcare.

Sadly, the bridge is empty. The role of policy makers is Organizational Leadership, keeping watch on the bridge ... where they are conspicuously absent. They have allowed themselves to be drawn into Operational Leadership, looking very much like the captain who spends his time in the engine room, telling the engineers what tools to use, what fuel to use, what mechanical interventions to perform, and what maintenance schedule to follow ... and then going to the ship's kitchen and doing the same—telling the cooks what meals to prepare, what ingredients to use, and what quantities to use. And in the meantime, there is no one on the bridge.

So, as the captain on the bridge, what is the government's role? It has four roles: to clarify and reinforce the purpose of healthcare, to clarify and reinforce the vision of healthcare, to reinforce the driving values for the overall healthcare delivery community, and to guard against abuse within the system—four roles which we clarify below.

- ***To clarify and reinforce the purpose of healthcare.***

   The job of policy makers and regulators is to promote and reinforce value for the patient. Value for the patient is created through better results at lower cost over time. And better results mean better outcomes, greater safety, higher satisfaction, greater access (in effect better service), and better patient functional capability.

   The government should reinforce the notion that the ultimate destination for healthcare is not just healing disease, but also preventing it. In Chapter Three, we made the distinction between four different levels of prevention: primary, secondary, tertiary, and quaternary prevention. The government should work to promote as much clarity as possible around all four:

   ○ ***Primary prevention***, the first line of prevention, is about preventing disease.

   ○ ***Secondary prevention*** is about preventing the disease from progressing to a high risk of death for the patient.

o *Tertiary prevention* is about helping people live well and conduct productive lives with their condition, which means eliminating avoidable and unnecessary doctor visits, hospital admissions, and visits to emergency departments.

o *Quaternary prevention* is about helping those who are acutely ill with chronic conditions, which means that when a patient does need urgent or acute care, it is delivered safely and at the right time—every time, with no waste.

The government should stimulate and encourage the system to address all four. That means promoting the kind of education that helps prevent disease as much as possible (primary and secondary prevention). Where efforts at primary and secondary prevention fail to prevent chronic diseases, the focus should then shift to tertiary prevention, and then to quaternary prevention. For tertiary and quaternary prevention, the government should:

o Ensure that value is being delivered and that payments are linked to that value, not merely a fee-for-services model for procedures done to and for patients.

o Foster transparency of results and costs.

o Promote the interoperability of information.

o Facilitate the flow of discovery from the knowledge domain to the care domain.

o Allow for learning from mistakes and near misses, without compromising the legitimate needs for compensation.

- *To clarify and reinforce the vision for healthcare.*

They need to promote the vision of high-quality, affordable healthcare for everyone and to then encourage the growth of the care delivery circle so that it absorbs more of the knowledge domain into its delivery. They need to make sure that the payer domain grows in tandem with the care delivery domain, providing the greatest possible overlap of their two circles—an overlap less about size and more about alignment with payments that link to outcomes, safety, service and overall costs over time ... in other words, an overlap that creates value.

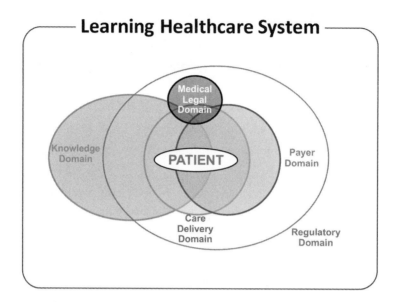

- *To reinforce the driving values for the overall healthcare delivery community.*

  Collaboration, transparency, and humility—their job is to keep reminding, reinforcing, and rewarding these values. If they do, the results will be spectacular. And they can start with a solid demonstration of these values on the floors and in the backrooms of the halls of policy creation.

- *To guard against abuse within the system.*

  Abuse is inevitable. Regulation is necessary. Their role is to require accountability, while remembering that accountability and micromanagement are not the same.

When policy makers and regulators fulfill their crucial roles well, they will make it much easier for healthcare providers to fulfill theirs. Instead of micromanagement, the health-policy and regulatory decisions they make that align with high-value healthcare will significantly facilitate the efforts of healthcare leaders to bring about the organizational changes we need to see in healthcare delivery ... which brings us to the role of healthcare providers.

The Role of Healthcare Providers

If policy makers and regulators don't exercise the kind of leadership we described above, it doesn't make it impossible for healthcare providers to exercise great leadership. But it does make it much more difficult.

There is in fact nothing stopping healthcare providers from pursuing the mission, vision, and values we have described. By doing so, they may well force the supporting stakeholders to follow their momentum.

So what does great leadership look like for healthcare providers?

Physicians are not taught to lead. They are taught to practice medicine. In this new climate, physicians need to do more than practice medicine. They need to lead. They haven't been trained to lead, and many have no inclination to lead. But to rescue healthcare, they will need to. As much as we are asking regulators to refocus their leadership, we may be asking physicians to do much more.

The fact is that the purpose, vision, and values outlined on these pages will never happen without their rising to the kind of leadership the purpose, vision, and values require.

So what do Organizational Leadership, Operational Leadership, and People Leadership look like on the frontlines?

Leadership Transitions

Careers are measured by transitions. They include transitions from one department to another, from one organization to another, and even from one career to another. But the most important—and least understood—transitions are these: the transitions of leadership.[29]

Over a typical career span, a typical professional will encounter five such critical leadership transitions. It might be four, it might be six, but these five transitions capture the most typical—and the most difficult—transitions a leader encounters over the course of a typical career:

---

29 We are indebted to the excellent work of Ram Charan, Steve Drotter, and Jim Noel for their work on these transitions. For an in-depth analysis, we recommend their book *The Leadership Pipeline: How to Build the Leadership Powered Company* (Jossey-Bass Second Edition 2011).

- Leading others (individual contributors)
- Leading those who lead others
- Leading a function
- Leading a business unit with multiple functions
- Leading an enterprise

These transitions are progressive, and they are captured in the diagram below.

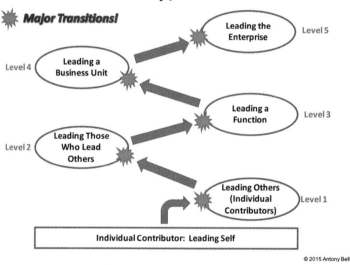

Critical Leadership/Career Transitions

We all start out our careers as individual contributors, where our only real responsibility is to lead ourselves: managing our time well, meeting deadlines, creatively addressing the problems within our sphere of responsibility, relating well to our peers, and figuring what our boss is looking for. Our focus is on our own personal productivity, and we are responsible for no one except ourselves.

But as we progress through life, times change …

Transition to Level 1

… And we come to the first promotion. We did well as individual contributors, well enough to be tapped on the shoulder for our first promotion into a leadership role—to Level 1. We most likely still perform some of the same work the team does and that we did before, but we are now responsible for the collective performance of this team. Our leadership focus is on execution—on Operational Leadership (the POM functions). This is often a difficult transition, because it requires a shift of mindset that only becomes more pronounced as our careers progress: ultimate success lies not in our own performance, but in the performance of those we lead. The better we performed as individual contributors, the harder the transition. The challenge of this transition is often compounded by the fact that we are now leading former peers.

Transition to Level 2

Somehow we master these challenges, and we are promoted again, this time to Level 2. This role requires us to lead a number of people doing what we did at Level 1: leading a group of individual contributors. This shift is a profound one, because it requires working almost entirely through other people—helping the leaders we lead to lead their people well. We are now further removed from the operations, at least in terms of direct execution, and our focus is now very developmental—helping these leaders be all they need to be in order to bring out the best in the people they lead. Our focus is heavily on the SEM functions of People Leadership. This is a particularly difficult transition because the extent of the shift is often unrecognized: it is assumed that Level 2 is the same as Level 1 (just more of it), and that if we performed well at Level 1, we will perform well at Level 2. Both are dangerous assumptions—the skills required at Level 2 are fundamentally different.

Transition to Level 3

Somehow we avoided falling for those erroneous assumptions, and we did well enough for a promotion to Level 3, leading a particular function—an operations unit, a functional department such as a finance unit or a clinical unit, for example. Now we are responsible not only for people leading people who lead others, but also for the overall performance for that particular function. At this level, our SEM functions remained the same, but now we assume more

Organizational Leadership responsibilities (the CAS functions), because we need to make sure that the function is aligned to the direction of the broader business unit we are part of, as well as to the direction of the whole organization itself. So to our SEM responsibilities are added significant CAS responsibilities. Our involvement in Operational Leadership is almost entirely focused on tracking the key performance metrics for our function and addressing any issues that couldn't be addressed by those we lead.

By this stage, it becomes obvious why leaders derail or become ineffective: they haven't let go of the Operational Leadership focus (the POM functions) that was inherent in their responsibilities at Level 1. They are trying to apply a Level 1 approach to a Level 3 responsibility.

Transition to Level 4

Again, we don't succumb, and again we are promoted, this time to Level 4. Now we are leading a business unit with multiple functions, and in many organizations, this means carrying the P&L (profit and loss) responsibility for the business unit. Our SEM responsibilities remain the same, but with a new twist: we are not only consciously and deliberately developing our direct reports (all of them leaders at levels 2 and 3), but we are also responsible for making sure that leadership development is part of the DNA of our business unit … that systems and processes are in place that support and push our leaders to develop themselves and to develop the leaders they lead. It's no longer enough to do it ourselves: we have to create the environment where all the leaders engage in leadership development.

To the SEM functions of Level 4 are added the CAS functions of Organizational Leadership. Our perspective at this level is largely external to the business unit—we are making sure that the business unit is aligned to the overall corporate direction and that we are working in concert and not at cross-purposes with other business units. In terms of Operational Leadership (POM), we keep a close eye on the key metrics, but our involvement in Operational Leadership is limited to addressing anything those metrics might surface that requires attention at our level.

Transition to Level 5

Well, the unexpected happens, and we are tapped on the shoulder to lead the entire enterprise ... we find ourselves at Level 5. Here the functions are similar to those at Level 4, but the audience is different. Now we are dealing with board members, regulators, unions, advocacy groups, investors, analysts, the local community, and other critical stakeholders. In terms of SEM, we are committed to developing the people on our team, but we are also now particularly concerned about making sure that we have adequate leadership bench strength at every level of the organization.

These levels are the most important and least appreciated transitions in a person's career. Their relationship to Organizational Leadership, Operational Leadership, and People Leadership is captured in the Leadership Cube™ below.

Critical Transitions and the Leadership Cube™

Transitions and the Organization

These transitions are critical for an individual, and they are equally critical for an organization.

According to the Corporate Executive Board, in a typical organization, those affected by all the transitions going on at any given time (the new leaders, direct reports, previous bosses, new bosses, and peers) represent nearly 45 percent of the employee population. When we consider that about 40 percent of the transitions are mishandled and the new leader at any level seriously underperforms, the impact on the organization is profound. Getting these transitions right is not only critical for an individual's career, it is also crucial for the overall performance of the organization.

This makes it all the more important that the supporting functions in your organization reinforce the multiple transitions going on from one leadership level to another. If you are in HR, training, organizational development, legal, IT, finance, or infrastructure, you sit on both sides of the diagram below: the five levels apply to you in your own career path, but you also have the added function of fulfilling your role in such a way that you contribute to the greatest number of smooth transitions from one level to the next. That's obviously true for HR and training, but it's equally true for IT, finance, infrastructure and all the rest. If you are in IT, for example, your underlying question is, "How can my IT services enhance the career transitions of the leaders I support? How can IT

Critical Leadership Transitions and Their Support Functions

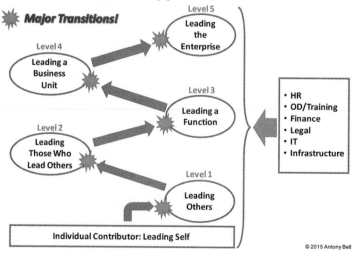

© 2015 Antony Bell

make them more effective?" You may not necessarily voice the question out loud, but framing what you do in these terms makes your contribution immeasurably more significant.

What happens when any of these transitions don't go well? Leaders end up skipping a level, whether they are prepared to or not.

Why does this happen? The simple and obvious answer is that leaders are in short supply, and many organizations put someone—sometimes anyone with a pulse—in a leadership role that needs to be filled, whether they are ready for it or not. And once in it, they are left to fend for themselves. It happens frequently in times of high growth or high turnover: individual contributors are thrust into Level 2 roles, those at Level 1 are put straight into Level 3 roles, and so on.

Bringing in someone from the outside isn't necessarily a solution either. If you are considering someone in a Level 3 role in another organization for a Level 3 role in yours, it's hard to know how well he or she actually fulfilled that Level 3 role and negotiated the transition into it. With the right questions, you can find out. You just need to make sure you ask them.

Healthcare Providers and the Leadership Transitions
For healthcare providers to exercise great leadership, they need to understand and negotiate these transitions well. If they do, their contribution to the transformation of healthcare will be profound. So how do they apply?

If you work in any kind of operational function—in hospital administration, for example—these levels will make intuitive sense to you. You can relate them to your own experience, and everyone else's. This explains why you may struggle at a particular level. It also explains how to make the most of your current leadership role. And if your responsibilities cover the entire organization (the entire hospital, for example) or a significant piece of it, this shows you how important it is to make sure that these transitions are well negotiated.

It isn't quite so simple for physicians. Hospital administrators are not expected to deliver their expertise as a billable good, but physicians are. Physicians are like lawyers and accountants—they run their own show and they also deliver their own goods.

For physicians, then, these transitions are particularly challenging. Their identity and sense of contribution is wrapped up in their effectiveness as an individual contributor. And precisely because they are effective, talented doctors are quickly promoted to Level 1 leadership roles. At Level 1, they can handle the tension between leading and practicing reasonably well. But above Level 1, the tension between the two becomes severe: not only are they wired to keep practicing, they are expected to. The leadership functions required by their roles inevitably suffer. They can find themselves at Level 3 exhausted, overworked and stressed—because they haven't understood the kind of leadership their role requires.

By and large, physicians see themselves as individual contributors; their sense of identity and validation comes from the expertise they have acquired at great effort and now dispense to their patients. So when they are put in leadership roles, they typically resent it because it takes them away from the delivery of their expertise. And when they are placed in a leadership role, many unconsciously see it as an opportunity to further the interests of their particular specialization.

The trends in healthcare force a resolution to this tension. The future of healthcare will not rest on individual expertise, but on collective expertise—the inevitable logic of both collaboration and transparency. The very mission and vision of healthcare rests on the resolution of this tension. We believe that the tension can be resolved. But resolving it requires two things of physicians: they need to acknowledge this tension, and they need to embrace the leadership responsibilities their leadership roles confer on them. Their role is now a function of both medical expertise *and* leadership capacity.

The Power of Ideas

If we stopped here, we might leave you with the impression that great leadership is a function of position and how well we negotiate the transition from one position to another.

But leadership is just as much about ideas. Two kinds of leadership co-exist in any kind of organization: leading from a position (direct), and leading with ideas (indirect).

The first is a functional leadership role with direct reports, often at multiple levels. The second may or may not have direct reports, but is nonetheless crucial to the direction of the organization. For example, research scientists in a chemical or pharmaceutical company may not have any direct reports, certainly not in comparison to an operational leader, but the influence they exert over the long-term success of the organization is enormous. Systems engineers reengineering the business processes of a complex delivery system may have few or no direct reports, but the influence of their leadership extends far beyond the confines of their title. These leaders exercise influence by virtue of the ideas and innovations they generate.

In reality, both direct and indirect leaders lead with the power of ideas and with the clarity of those ideas. If you have few or no direct reports, your challenge is to persuade ... and this is just as true even if you do have direct reports. You may be in a functional leadership role, but your success depends on how well you communicate the ideas and principles that will create the success of your organization or unit.

Ideas are powerful. And great leaders articulate them well—thoughtfully and deliberately.

This truth underscores the tremendously important role that physicians play. The extent to which they embrace and propagate the mission, vision, and values of healthcare will be the extent to which the mission, vision and values take root.

And Now to *Character* in Leadership ...

Congratulations ... you have covered some critical material on great leadership! We have addressed in some depth one wing of the aircraft—*competence* in leadership. Now let's address the other wing—*character* in leadership—and its critical role in the transformation of healthcare.

Chapter 13

What is Character in Leadership?

C ompetence, we have said, gets us to the table. But it's character that keeps us there.

Great leadership is impossible without strong character. Without it, a leader can still accomplish much, but it won't result in game-changing leadership. How we lead people (character) is as important as where we lead them (competence).

Having said that, we should probably take some time to define character. So what *is* character? And what *isn't* character?

Character and Personality

Character and personality are not the same, though people often confuse the two. Each of us is born with a certain personality, which essentially doesn't change, even though the events of life can certainly modify it. If you were asked to describe someone's personality, you would most likely use words like gregarious, shy, talkative, outgoing, reserved, meticulous, disorganized, organized, and so on and so forth.

If you were asked to describe someone's *character*, you would most likely use a different set of words, words that conjure up qualities like trust, reliability, dependability, integrity, honesty, and courage (or their opposites). Given the time, you would most likely create a pretty substantial list. In a previous chapter we learned about Xenophon's list of thirteen qualities—and his list is by no means exhaustive.

While character is more about the choices we make, personality is more about what we are born with. Someone who is naturally gregarious will not suddenly become shy, but both a gregarious person and a shy person can both make courageous decisions, they can both be dependable, and they can both be honest and trustworthy—and both can be their opposite.

The Qualities of Character

Which brings us back to character: How do we make sense of all the different character qualities that appear on the kinds of lists that Xenophon compiled?

…With the Pyramid of Personal Qualities.

Just like any other edifice, the durability of the Pyramid of Personal Qualities depends on four critical elements:

1. A strong foundation
2. A solid superstructure

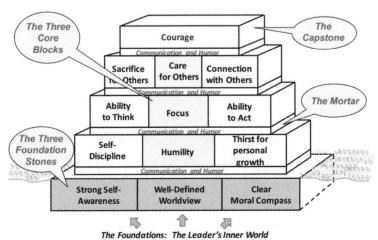

The Character Side of Great Leadership

The Foundations: The Leader's Inner World

© 2014 LeaderDevelopment Inc.

3. The right material to hold it all together

4. And a capstone

This pyramid would simply crumble without any one of these elements. The same is true with character in leadership.

The pyramid's bedrock has three foundational stones. The superstructure above the foundation is built and anchored around three building blocks that provide the core and the backbone of the structure. Each of the building blocks is held together with mortar, and the entire structure is capped with a capstone. Let's look at these four elements in turn.

1. The Foundations of the Pyramid

A building is only as strong as its foundation. If the foundation is weak, it doesn't matter how strong the superstructure is; with a weak foundation, it will eventually collapse. The structure in this case is built on three solid foundation stones:

1. Self-awareness

2. A well-defined worldview

3. A clear moral compass

These foundation stones are critical to great leadership, whatever the task or organization you lead.

Self-Awareness

All the great leaders we encounter in the marketplace have one thing in common: they have huge amounts of self-awareness. They know their own strengths and weaknesses, but more than that, they know their inner passions and aspirations. They know what they value, and they reflect on what is important to them. Without that deep sense of self-awareness, great leadership is elusive. If it happens, it is accidental and fleeting.

To build this kind of self-awareness, we should engage in habits great leaders engage in, however unfamiliar and unpracticed these habits may feel. Three are particularly important:

- Great leaders embrace feedback. They not only graciously receive feedback, they also actively seek it. If you have spinach in your teeth, you want someone to tell you. Feedback takes many forms, some formal (feedback instruments, reviews) and some informal (one-on-one conversations). Whatever the form, great leaders seek out such feedback.

- Great leaders reflect on what's important to them. We need to know the values we embrace. Great leaders keep a journal, and use it to clarify their thoughts, reflect on events, record important conversations, and capture key observations.

- Most of all, great leaders are committed to growth and self-development. For them, self-awareness is an essential tool for such growth.

Consider the impact on a hospital if feedback were not only willingly given, but also eagerly sought. What would it do to safety statistics? To the patient experience? To the working relationship among doctors, and between doctors and administrators? To the overall effectiveness of the hospital?

Well-Defined Worldview

Healthy self-awareness demands a clear, well-articulated worldview. But what do we mean by a worldview? Very simply, it's how we view the world around us, or the immediate world in which we reside. It's the explanation we give about life and how we make a sense of it. A worldview is the set of beliefs that we hold and the assumptions that we make (sometimes consciously but often unconsciously) about how the world around us works, and how we can succeed in that world.

It's a *mental map* that helps us make sense of the contours of the terrain around us and a map that helps us decide what choice we make at each crossroad. Our worldview is the pair of glasses we put on every morning, through which we filter life as we experience it throughout the day.

Where does our worldview come from? It is shaped and formed by multiple influences:

- *Our cultural, national context.* Growing up in America is different from growing up in India or China, or Brazil or Argentina or South Africa, or France or Greece or Russia or the UK.

- *Our particular ethnic background.* Growing up as Irish Catholic in Boston is different from growing up as Mexican immigrant in Texas, or an African American in Mississippi, or a Pakistani in London, or an Algerian in Paris.

- *Our educational background.* My (Antony) education through high school was mostly in France and the UK, and it no doubt shaped me differently than if I had gone to a school in the US or Turkey or Mozambique.

- *The people who had an impact on us.* Parents, grandparents, teachers, coaches, uncles, aunts, and so on.

- *The major ideas and concepts that have influenced us.* Have you ever read a book that profoundly resonated with you and changed your thinking? That book influenced your worldview. These ideas and concepts include our religious beliefs, as well as our views on human nature, human destiny, and meaning in life. At some point, we reach some conclusions, and those conclusions shape our worldview.

- *The significant events we have experienced.* I (Antony) recently heard a speech by Hedy Epstein in which she recounted the painful experience as an eight-year-old when her parents put her on a train to the UK from Germany. It was just before the outbreak of World War II, and she never saw her parents again. They later died in a German concentration camp. An event like that has a profound impact—here she is in her 70s and she is still defined by it.

- *Our own preferences and behavioral styles.* The way we are wired clearly has an impact because it determines how we react to these influences.

Deciphering Worldview … From a Well-Placed Kick

A senior vice president at one of our client's companies once strode into a meeting, and somewhere between the door and his chair announced that his right leg was "sore from kicking everyone in the rear end all day!" (His language was stronger and more colorful.)

I (Antony) wasn't at that meeting, but I had two thoughts when I was told about it: The first was, "I'm glad I wasn't at that meeting!" And the second was: "That's his worldview!" That single statement exposed his leadership philosophy, and more significantly, the worldview that shaped the leadership philosophy supporting it.

What Drives a Leader's Behaviors?

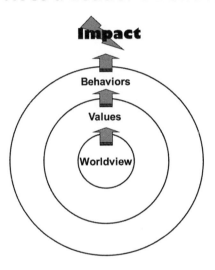

In that one statement, he revealed what he thought about people, about individual contribution, about motivation, and about his role as a leader—and all these defined the way he behaved as a leader. In his own worldview, he saw people as lazy, unmotivated, and untrustworthy, and the only way to get the best out of them was with a well-placed kick. His behavior—going around delivering well-placed kicks—was a direct product of his worldview.

Now contrast that worldview with the worldview of other leaders who see people as essentially self-motivated, and when given the right conditions and the right incentives, will inherently want to do their best. These leaders don't lead by fear and intimidation, but by creating the kind of environment that encourages them to offer their best. They prefer an arm on the shoulder rather than a foot in the backside.

But notice something that both kinds of leaders have in common: they both share the common value of wanting their people to perform at their best. The difference is in the worldview that shapes the pursuit of that value and the behaviors to achieve it: for the senior VP, it means going around delivering well-placed kicks, and for the others, it means placing an arm on a shoulder and looking for ways to enhance the inner motivation they believe exists within the people they lead.

So why is a leader's worldview important to his or her leadership?

- Your worldview is at the heart of who you are. It shapes your values, and defines what you consider important.
- Those values then shape your behavior.
- Behavior is a function of your worldview and values. They shape your assumptions about how people learn, how they work, how they are motivated, and how you should lead them. If you are uncomfortable with some of your behaviors as a leader, you need to explore the worldview and values that are driving them.

Your worldview matters: it shapes the way you lead.

Consider the impact on a hospital where its leaders, both medical and administrative, operate from a worldview that is not only clear and well articulated, but also widely embraced and applied. What would that do to the sense of unity, cohesion, and to decision-making? What would it do for safety statistics? For the patient experience? For the working relationship among and between the various providers, such as the doctors, nurses, and administrators? For the profitability of the hospital? We can all agree the impact would be substantial.

A Clear Moral Compass

Our VP with the sore right leg also tells us something else: not all worldviews are created equal. Some are clearly better than others, and the better worldviews are those that follow a clear moral compass. Every leader has a worldview, but not all leaders build theirs on a clear moral foundation. Hitler and Stalin, and many others like them, had a clear worldview, but theirs were anything but moral, and the leadership edifice they built eventually collapsed.

Again, consider for a moment the impact on a hospital where its leaders, both medical and administrative, operate from a set of moral values that are generally and widely embraced. What would it do to the sense of unity and cohesion? What would it do to decision-making? What would it do to safety statistics? To the patient experience? To the working relationship among and between providers? To the profitability of the hospital?

2. The Core

Three building blocks form the core of the pyramid:

1. Humility
2. Focus
3. Care for others

These three pillars are the backbone of the superstructure. All the other blocks tie into these three core concepts.

Humility

Humility is defined as putting the interests of those we lead and the interests of the organization above our own. It may not be a word we'd typically associate with leadership, and yet, it is transformational. This is not a self-esteem issue: as we have said before, it's not so much a question of thinking less *of* ourselves, but rather a question of thinking less *about* ourselves.

Humility is rare in leaders, but it's powerful when it's there. It's powerful because it's disarming. There is a certain selflessness in this characteristic of great leadership. And the antithesis of humility is arrogance. The Greeks had a special word for it: hubris, and the word actually means excessive arrogance, based on a misplaced self-confidence. In Greek tragedy, it was hubris that was invariably the undoing of a leader, and it always preceded a catastrophic fall.

|||||||||||||||||||||||||||||||||||||||||||||||||||||||||||||||||||||||||||||||||||||||||||||||||||||||||||||||||||||||||||||||||||||||||||||||||||||||||||||||||||||||||||||

Hubris and Humility (Antony)

There's a high likelihood you've seen hubris in action. I witnessed one instance that profoundly marked me when I was working for a Dutch brokerage firm, running the office in Eastern France. I had a counterpart in Paris who led, somewhat to my envy, a thriving and prosperous operation. On one of my visits to Paris, I happened to be in his office when he pulled off one of his more spectacular deals. To those of us assembled with him, he proclaimed, "Maintenant on sait qu'on connaît bien notre métier" (Now we know we have mastered our business). But within months, he and his staff experienced some significant setbacks, and one year later the office was closed down, a casualty of his own hubris. It was a sobering spectacle.

I have also witnessed the antithesis of this hubris. One involved an executive I worked for whose superiors felt he needed to move on to something different, and hand over his role to someone with different strengths. He was very entrepreneurial and creative, and he felt his strengths were still needed. But what unfolded was one of the most vivid examples of humility—from both parties—I have ever witnessed. This would normally have been a confrontation of two strong leaders posturing for the same position, but the one who was being replaced set out, as he put it, to "prove himself wrong," despite very real misgivings. And the one coming in came in with a spirit of servant leadership. As he put it, "There's always room for another servant." Remarkably, the transition turned out to be the best transition of its kind that the organization had ever seen, thanks to the humility of the two leaders involved. Both leaders put the interests of the organization above their own, and in the process, their stature as leaders was substantially enhanced.

|||||||||||||||||||||||||||||||||||||||||||||||||||||||||||||||||||||||||||||||||||||||||||||||||||||||||||||||||||||||||||||||||||||||||||||||||||||||||||||||||||||||||||||

The two blocks that accompany humility—self-discipline and the thirst for personal growth—are two qualities that reinforce that humility. When you find this kind of humility in leaders—the humility that puts the interests of their people and the interests of the organization ahead of their own—you will find self-discipline and a thirst to grow and learn. Humility teaches us that we have much to learn, and knowing that we have much to learn helps us impose the discipline to learn.

Focus

Great leaders maintain intense focus. Focus is about passion, but passion doesn't mean extravert exuberance. A leader can be an introvert, and still be a passionate, focused leader. It has to do with perseverance and discipline more than personality. Jim Collins uncovered this quality in leaders that took companies from good to great (the other one he identified, by the way, was humility).[30]

At one time a friend had a sign outside his office door that read, "Keep the main thing the main thing." Someone took a pen and changed it to read, "Keep the 23 main things the 23 main things." He actually never changed this graffiti, because whoever made the change made a great point: it's actually very difficult to maintain our focus. And yet focus is one of the core qualities of great leaders. Churchill once observed that a bulldog's snout is slanted backwards so that it can keep breathing without letting go. As Collins indicated, this focus is a tenacious commitment to the cause that knows no deterrent.

Focus is your ability not only to articulate a clear sense of direction, but also to keep everyone else's focus on that direction. Without that focus, an organization is rudderless. And without it, the ability to think and the ability to act (the two building blocks that go with it) have no context. However decisive a leader may be, however developed his or her ability to think, such qualities are meaningless without this focus. But with this focus, the ability to think and the ability to act have context and substance.

Care for Others

Care for others is just as important as humility and focus. If you don't genuinely care for the well-being of those you lead, you're not going to exercise great leadership. You can still get things done, but without that care for your people, you'll never achieve the level of greatness that you can if you do care for them.

---

30   See *Good to Great*, Jim Collins

Care for others is not the same as being nice or gentle to the people you lead. Don't confuse the two. Great leaders genuinely care for the people they lead, but that doesn't mean they are always nice or gentle to them. Doctors sometimes inflict pain on their patients for their own good. And consider great wartime generals, whatever the war and whatever the era: the ones whose troops were most loyal were those who believed that their general cared about what mattered most to them—their survival. So they put up with long and grueling marches to gain some advantage that would ensure their victory—and their survival. These generals weren't particularly gentle with their soldiers, but they did care for them. And their soldiers loved them because of it.

Now don't take this as a license to be ugly and demeaning to the people you lead. But do take this to mean that your primary concern is their growth and development, not their comfort. It means you care about their success, because that's what matters to them.

The two accompanying blocks—sacrifice for others and connection with them—are like the others: logical and intuitively appropriate. If we care for them, we will sacrifice for them and take pains to communicate well with them. You may have heard of the term "Emotional Intelligence," or EQ—well, that's what this is about.

3. The Mortar

Communication and humor are the mortar that holds it all together. Communication is the ability to articulate ideas clearly, concisely, and creatively. It's the ability to paint pictures with words. Communication is a creative process that requires thought and preparation.

In the movie *Dead Poets Society*, Robin Williams plays the role of a teacher at a New England private boarding school. More than anything else, he wants to inculcate in them the courage to think differently, to risk thinking differently. In the most memorable scene of the movie, he takes the entire class into a hallway filled with trophies and rows of group photos of the school's alumni, many of them long dead. Pressing his cheek to the glass case, with a voice full of intensity, he asks them, "Can you hear what they're saying?" And in a hoarse whisper, he breathes out, *Carpe diem!* (*Seize the day!*). Now he could just as easily have given the same message from the front of the classroom, but instead he chose to communicate his message in a way they would never forget.

Communication is not only about *how* we communicate; it's also about *what* we communicate. In fact, the key to clear communication is clear ideas. Creativity is important, but substance is even more important. Substance creates authenticity. To communicate well you have to have ideas—that's why we spent time talking about your worldview and your values.

Reagan was called the great communicator, but he was a great communicator because he had clear ideas. Before he was elected to the presidency, he asked Richard Allen (who later became his first national security advisor) if he would like to hear his theory on the Cold War. "Some people think I'm simplistic," Reagan told him, "but there's a difference between being simplistic and being simple. My theory of the Cold War is that we win and they lose. What do you think about that?" Richard Allen was completely taken aback by the power and simplicity of the idea. As he later reflected, "I'd worked for Nixon and Goldwater and many others, and I'd heard a lot about … détente and the need to 'manage the Cold War,' but never did I hear a politician put the goal so starkly." For all Reagan's giftedness as a communicator, he was far more a man of ideas; the clarity of his ideas simply made them easy to communicate. Without clear ideas, communication is empty words. The point is a simple one: if you are clear on your ideas, you'll find ways to communicate them creatively.

A quick word about humor: isn't it interesting how much we like people who make us laugh? Leaders who make us laugh are no exception. And perhaps that's the difference between the great leaders we admire and the ones we love: the ones we love, we love because they make us laugh, and because they make us laugh, we want to be around them.

Think of some of the great leaders of the past—people like Lincoln and Churchill. They were both great men, and in their different ways, great leaders, but they had in common a keen sense of humor. Doris Kearns Goodwin describes Lincoln as possessing "a remarkable sense of humor and a gift for storytelling that allowed him to defuse tensions and relax his colleagues at difficult moments. Many of his stories, taken from his seemingly limitless stock, were directly applicable to a point being argued. Many were self-deprecatory, all were hilarious."

We remember Churchill's inspiring words, but we remember his humor even more. He had this extraordinary ability to come back with the perfect quip. On one occasion at a dinner party Lady Astor—a political opponent—was sitting next to him, and she said to him, "You know, Winston, if I were married to you, I'd put poison in your soup." Without a pause, Churchill replied, "You know, Nancy, if I were married to you, I'd drink it."

We remember Reagan for his humor. When he went into the operating room after being shot from an attempted assassination, he looked up at the doctors about to operate on him, and said, "I sure hope you are all Republicans!" We are endeared to someone who in the heat of the moment can lighten our emotions.

4. The Capstone

The capstone, the fitting conclusion to these personal qualities of leadership, is courage. Churchill considered courage as "the first of human qualities, because it is the quality which guarantees all others." As CS Lewis[31] put it, "Courage is not simply one of the virtues, but the form of every virtue at the testing point."

They are right: courage is the one virtue that gives life to all the others. What is the value of a clear moral compass, if we don't have the courage to live by it? What is focus, if we lack the courage to make the tough choices? What is care for others if we don't have the courage to express it?

We tend to associate courage with physical or political courage. We think of the stand of the Spartans at Thermopylae in 480 BC, a mere 300 in the face of a Persian army that numbered hundreds of thousands, and by some estimates, over a million. All three hundred died, but their stand rallied the city-states of Greece who later defeated the Persians and changed the course of history. Or we think of the defenders of the Alamo, or Edith Cavell, a hospital administrator in Belgium who hid and evacuated fleeing allied soldiers during World War I, or Raoul Wallenberg rescuing Jews in Nazi-occupied Hungary, or Dietrich Bonhoeffer, a German pastor who joined the covert resistance to Hitler … all of them doing what they did at the cost of their lives. Or we think of the signers

---

31   Oxford University Professor in the last century, prolific author on English literature, history, Christian apologetics, as well as fiction (best known for *The Chronicles of Narnia*); friend and contemporary of J.R.R. Tolkien (*Lord of the Rings*).

of the Declaration of Independence, who may not have lost their lives, but they knew they were signing a death warrant if their cause failed.

Inspiring though these men and women are, they don't reflect the kind of courage we need in the marketplace and in healthcare. It may be less visible and less spectacular, but it's just as critical. In fact, the older we get the more convinced we are of its critical role in great leadership. We work with many leaders to help them apply great leadership to their organization, and inevitably, at some point, they are confronted with a choice that requires courage. Some of them respond; some of them don't. When they don't, it really doesn't matter what other virtues they have. Their virtues become irrelevant when courage fails them, and these same virtues stand tall when courage reinforces them.

So what does courage look like in healthcare, whatever your role as a stakeholder? We'd like to suggest five ways that you display courage:

1. The courage to know yourself
2. The courage to put the interests of others ahead of your own
3. The courage to confront others
4. The courage to align the organization to its true direction
5. The courage to draw a moral line in the sand

1. The Courage to Know Yourself

Courage is the willingness to look inside. It's the willingness to acknowledge what we see inside—not just our strengths and talents, but also our weaknesses, our insecurities, and our struggles. We typically don't associate self-awareness with courage, but it takes courage to be authentic, and courage to ask ourselves the tough questions about ourselves. Courage is the hallmark of self-discovery and self-awareness.

It takes courage to receive feedback, and the test of whether we have this courage is our willingness to ask for and listen to it. Leaders who don't embrace feedback are, deep down, afraid of what the feedback might reveal. It requires courage to face our weaknesses, and it takes courage to listen to people telling us about them. Perhaps that's what Churchill meant when he said, "Courage is what it takes to stand up and speak; courage is also what it takes to sit down and listen." One of the curious inconsistencies of marketplace leadership is that many leaders insist on their people being open to feedback while at the same time feeling exempt from the same kind of scrutiny. By contrast, great leaders set the pace for this kind of scrutiny.

The courage to know ourselves also helps us to be courageous in other areas. The courage to select people who are stronger and more gifted than ourselves, for example, is impossible without a strong dose of self-awareness. When Lincoln appointed as cabinet ministers three of his rivals in the Republican primaries—William Henry Seward, Salmon Chase, and Edward Bates, all three better educated and, in virtually everyone's mind (and certainly in their own), better qualified for the office—he took the political community by surprise and was roundly condemned for a naïve and foolish move. But it was above all a courageous act, and his secretary, John Nicolay, later wrote that Lincoln's "first decision was one of great courage and self-reliance." Great leaders have the courage to select talent greater than their own, and the greater their courage in knowing themselves, the greater their courage in selecting such talent.

2. The Courage to Put the Interests of Others Ahead of Our Own

Courage requires making sacrifices for those we lead. Placing their interests above our own takes courage. Getting involved in the growth and development of the people we lead is a messy business, and it takes a measure of courage to roll up our sleeves and thrust our hands in the dirt. We will at times be disappointed, but courage keeps us going anyway. It takes courage to invest in their lives, and courage to stick out our necks for them, giving them challenging assignments, knowing that the risk of their failure may reflect poorly on us. It takes courage to stretch them and demand more from them, not mindlessly, but appropriately. Courage tells us to do it anyway.

3. The Courage to Confront Others

Difficult conversations where you address the needs or adverse behaviors of the people you lead, are, well, difficult. They are nonetheless very necessary. If you genuinely care for the people you lead, you will have those tough conversations. But however beneficial and important we know they are, it still takes courage to have them. They are never easy, but they are critical. And engaging in those conversations requires courage.

4. The Courage to Align the Organization to Its True Direction

Defining and clarifying the purpose, vision, and values of an organization is the easy part.

The hard part is making those alignment decisions that make sure the organization is in step with the mission, vision, and values. That, at times, takes courage.

Several years ago, we spent more than two years helping a major player in its field embed deep into the organization a commitment to its new direction. We worked with 80 of the organization's key leaders, and it was very successful—it raised morale and generated considerable excitement around the new direction. But it all unraveled when the senior leaders never made the alignment decisions critical to the new direction. Initiatives that should have been eliminated were left intact, money was still allocated to projects that didn't match the new direction, powerful internal leaders, whose vested interest lay in the original status quo, went unchallenged, and leaders who should have been shifted to new responsibilities were never reassigned. All these alignment decisions needed to be made, but weren't … all because of an absence of courage in the leadership—the courage to align the organization to its true direction. The very success of the first part (embedding the new direction deep within the organization) made it even worse, because it raised expectations that ended up being sorely disappointed. The impact was huge. Morale sank, and whoever had the opportunity to leave did. All because of the absence of courage.

We see this happening all too often around us, and you no doubt have your own stories. We see organizational leaders asking staff to develop a new model of medical delivery, or a new surgical program, or a new research program. The staff assigned the task start out as skeptics, but as the project progresses, they begin to believe that something new will actually happen. They become engaged, and then enthused, as they actually see a path to success. But then some structural or organizational or operational policy change is initiated, which handicaps the project. At this point, senior organizational leaders are required to make a change, and protecting the project requires courage. When the organizational leaders fail to do their part, morale sinks, and in a frequently passive-aggressive fashion, skepticism settles back in again. All because of the organizational leaders' lack of courage.

5. The Courage to Draw the Line in the Sand

Courage is acting on principle, not poll. It's being willing to be unpopular, swimming against the current for what we hold as right. In politics, those stands are generally widely visible. In the private sector they usually aren't. But we still face the same kind of choices, albeit not as spectacular. They only become spectacular when the courageous choices are not made. Enron and many others became spectacular examples, not because they drew the line in the sand, but because they failed to. In the end, the fall of Enron was the product of a lack of courage ... the courage to take a stand on unethical behavior. The same could be said for the many players involved in creating the complex and questionable financial instruments that so significantly contributed to the financial and economic turmoil at the end of the last decade.

This brings us back to the importance of clarity around our worldview and the importance of having a clear moral compass. As we discussed back then, that means an acceptance of absolutes, at least at some level. When we draw a line in the sand, we are saying that one side of the line is right and the other side is wrong, and that inherently implies absolutes. No great leader was ever a relativist. Lincoln staked his leadership on the fact that slavery was wrong, however much those engaged in it told him it was none of his business.

So it means taking a stand, and to take a stand, we need to know why we are standing. That means sculpting a clear worldview and a crystal clear sense of our moral compass, which is important because at some point you will be confronted with choices that inevitably have a moral or ethical dimension to them. You may even have to confront evil, and that takes courage. Such choices are made before you are confronted with them, and it's beforehand that you need to decide what your response will be. If you find that someone has been doing something morally wrong, how will you react? If you discover your leadership is engaged in some kind of abusive practice, what will you do? If you see someone mistreated and unfairly handled, will you speak up? You don't make the right decision on the spot unless you have given thought to where you draw the line in the sand—*before* you get into the heat of the moment.

In the next chapter, we apply the principles of character in leadership to healthcare—and to your own particular critical role, whatever your role as a stakeholder. But before we do, take a moment to consider these questions:

- How important is character in leadership in meeting the challenges of healthcare?
- Which of these qualities are particularly important?
- Where or how have they been present?
- Where or how have they been absent?
- For your own leadership, which of these character qualities speak to you particularly?

Armed with your answers, it's time to address this critical question: *How will character in leadership transform healthcare?* That is the subject of the next chapter.

Chapter 14

How Will Character in Leadership Transform Healthcare?

T his may well be the most important chapter in the book. Everything else we discussed to this point stands or falls on the message found within this chapter.

How important is character for a leader in healthcare?

It is so important that if the answer is not emphatically and passionately, "vitally important!" then there will be no meaningful, lasting reform. That emphatic and impassioned response should come from every stakeholder—or at least from enough key stakeholders to create the right kind of momentum and the right kind of critical mass.

In earlier chapters, we explored the meaning of competence in leadership. As important as it is, competence alone will not rescue healthcare. Competence devoid of character is the well-run slave trade, the well-oiled drug cartel, the cold efficiency of the gas chambers, the ruthlessly predatory prostitution ring ... as well as any legitimate enterprise where the interests of the end-users and the well-being of those who serve them are subsumed by some to meet their own personal ambitions and interests.

So character in healthcare really *does* matter. But what does it look like?

The Empty Table

Imagine a large table filled with representatives of every stakeholder. Next to the healthcare providers and administrators sit the business interests in healthcare. Opposite them both sit the policy makers and regulators, flanked by healthcare educators on one side and the legal profession on the other.

The table itself is empty, with its deep mahogany finish fully exposed. Where does everyone focus with nothing on the table? Naturally, they look at the unobstructed view of the other people around the table. And as they look at one another, suspicions surface, accusations are made, fingers are pointed, and voices are raised … until they have had enough, and each one, slowly or abruptly, leaves the table.

The Objects on the Table

The debate would be different if they weren't discussing around an empty table. If the table were filled with useful objects, the focus would be on the objects on the table, not on the people around the table. So if we imagine that scenario, what goes on the table?

The Character Side of Great Leadership

The Foundations: The Leader's Inner World

© 2014 LeaderDevelopment Inc.

Five objects ... and they all have to do with character:

1. *A common worldview*—agreement on fundamental principles of ends and means.
2. *A commitment to humility*—a willingness to listen and debate in such a way that everyone can buy into the pursuit of the greater good.
3. *A shared focus*—a shared commitment to a common vision.
4. *A high value on care for others*—a common commitment to the care of the ultimate beneficiaries of healthcare and all those who serve them.
5. *And courage*—a mutually reinforced commitment to courageous action.

These five tenets are central to character in leadership and are captured in the Character Pyramid we discussed in the last chapter.

Unpacking the Objects

These five objects apply to everyone around the table ... but how? Let's unpack each one, and then take a look at the different stakeholders to see which of these five objects apply most directly.

A Common Worldview

If we had to pick the one single fact that, more than any other, shapes how leaders lead, it would be the clarity and articulation of their worldview. Their worldview inevitably determines their leadership prowess. Worldview defines goals, priorities, values, and relationships.

In the previous chapter, we defined worldview as the set of beliefs we hold and the assumptions we make, sometimes consciously and often unconsciously, about how the world around us works and how we can succeed in that world.

Our worldview determines every decision we make and every action we take. If you are baffled by the actions of a leader, uncover his or her worldview, and you will no longer be baffled. Before you vote, read whatever that person has written, and you will not be surprised by the choices they make.

Every conflict is ultimately a conflict of worldviews. The global conflicts of the past hundred years have been conflicts of ideologically opposed worldviews, whether the Allies against Hitler, the West against the Soviet Union, or the West against radical Islam. At a more benign level, but no less potent, is the conflict of corporate cultures in the marketplace. This clash of cultures explains why so many mergers fail: they cannot reconcile the very different worldviews deeply embedded in each culture. The inevitable result is enforced assimilation by one over the other—or eventually, separation. Daimler-Benz's acquisition of Chrysler ended in separation for that very reason: their worldviews were fundamentally too different, and ultimately irreconcilable. It became clear the alliance was doomed when a group of engineers from both sides spent a whole week arguing about the size and color of a brochure. They weren't arguing about the size and color of a brochure; they were unwittingly competing over which worldview would win.

For a lasting and profound transformation of healthcare delivery, every stakeholder's worldview should overlap with certain key beliefs and convictions such as:

- Collaboration is good
- No one has all the answers
- Compromise may produce a better outcome
- Honest, respectful debate is healthy
- Moral standards are important

There are no doubt others, but if these are not present, the stakeholders won't even sit down at the same table. No one will *listen* to each other.

In healthcare today, we have a clash of leadership worldviews that mirrors a similar clash elsewhere in the marketplace: the clash between Cicero and Machiavelli.

Cicero was one of the greatest men produced by the Roman Empire. Born in 106 BC, he lived through a crucial time when the Roman Empire experienced a dramatic and turbulent transition from a democratic republic to a dictatorship under the Caesars. He fought for the ideals of the republic, and despite the unsuccessful efforts of Caesar Augustus to win him over, Cicero's opposition cost him his life. Shortly before his death in 43 BC, he wrote a treatise on leadership called *On Moral Duties*. It was actually addressed to his son, a student in Athens, and his premise was simple: you *can* succeed as a great leader by doing the right thing. Success as a leader and moral integrity are not incompatible; in fact, Cicero argued, immoral acts, even for legitimate ends, will in the end come back to haunt you.

Throughout the Middle Ages, *On Moral Duties* was considered the benchmark for leadership … until some fifteen centuries later when, in 1513, Nicolo Machiavelli penned *The Prince* as a conscious and deliberate refutation of *On Moral Duties*.

It's hard to imagine a greater contrast to Cicero than Machiavelli. He argued that no act of leadership is immoral; it can only be judged by whether it works or not. It is not immoral if it works. In effect, the leader is above the law. He is exempt and can do what he wants. When David Frost interviewed President Nixon after the Watergate scandal in the seventies, the most revealing moment came when Nixon said, "When the President does it, it's not a crime." Nixon had put himself above the law. Machiavelli would have agreed with him—and applauded him. His sole criticism would have been that Nixon got caught.

Machiavelli's advice to leaders is this:

- A strong leader is cruel and ruthless. It's better to be feared than to be loved.
- A strong leader is cunning. Use fall guys; let them take the blame, turn on them, and take the credit for eliminating them.
- A strong leader lies. Everyone expects a leader to lie, so lie anyway. Lie when it's necessary or expedient, and don't worry whether people believe you or not.
- A strong leader is guarded. Be careful who advises you, and be specific about the advice you are looking for. The more you take advice, the more you lose control.
- A strong leader is stingy. There is no value in generosity.

Virtues, Machiavelli argued, may be preferable, but we operate in a world where virtues are impracticable. We're better off dispensing with them. Given the choice between a virtue and its corresponding vice, go for the vice—you'll be more effective as a leader.

This may seem like a caricature, but it isn't. The five qualities championed by Machiavelli are the almost exact antithesis of the convictions we identified earlier as critical for healthcare:

1. Collaboration is good
2. No one has all the answers
3. Compromise may produce a better outcome
4. Honest, respectful debate is healthy
5. Moral standards are important

The Prince, better translated as *The Leader,* became tremendously influential—from Henry VIII in England (a contemporary) all the way to Hitler and Stalin and on to the present day, where his voice remains strong and clear. Machiavellianism is alive and well. Especially so in the marketplace: he wrote one of the first modern self-help books on leadership, and many of the current self-help books in airports and bookstores are echoes of Machiavelli—unwittingly and unconsciously perhaps, and more muted, but nonetheless following the trail blazed by Machiavelli.

We need a leadership worldview shaped by Cicero, not Machiavelli. We need to embrace the virtues of collaboration, discourse, honesty, respect, and moral integrity. If Machiavelli's worldview shapes the discourse, there will be no rescuing healthcare.

A Commitment to Humility

Genuine humility will not lag far behind if we can come to a common worldview and a general buy-in into the five qualities of healthcare we describe above. If so, we are more likely to find common ground. We are more likely to build trust. And in finding common ground, we are more likely to listen, and then adjust. We will be more willing to make some concessions in the interests of the greater good. We are much more likely to engage with humility.

In the previous chapter, we defined humility as putting the interests of those we lead and the interests of the organization above our own (we could add to these the interests of the patient and the interests of the whole of healthcare as a sector). This shows us that humility isn't about self-esteem. As we mentioned, it's not about thinking less *of* ourselves, but about thinking less *about* ourselves—and more about those we lead and serve.

Some may argue that it requires a certain level of humility to build a common worldview—that humility actually precedes worldview rather than follows it. That is true: it requires a certain level of humility to even shape a common worldview. But the deeper levels of humility—really working for the interests of those we lead and for the greater good—are much more likely to happen if that common worldview has been established.

So what does humility look like for everyone around the table?

- Recognizing that everyone has a boss—even the boss.
- Being committed to a much greater good than our own personal interests.
  - In healthcare, being committed to the best interests of the patient and to the general health of the broader population.
- Having a keen sense of our own vulnerability to the sin of hubris.
  - Knowing that success and advancement can blind us to what can derail us.
- Acknowledging that at times we are followers of those we lead.
- Attaching more importance to the success of those we lead and to the success of the organization than we do to our own success—and to the broader success for the whole of healthcare.
  - Knowing that our own success is ultimately only measured by our ability to make others successful.
- Being deeply committed to lifelong learning.
  - Knowing that we never stop learning, however extensive our experience becomes.

- Taking firm positions...
    - On principle, not on pride.
    - On the good of the organization and its people, not on self-interest and personal advancement.
- Knowing that we have, like everyone else, disruptive and destructive tendencies that require self-discipline to curb—and openness to the feedback that exposes them.

A Shared Focus

Focus is about priorities. It assumes that we know what's important and what isn't. Focus helps us establish priorities. It assumes we know where to, well, *focus*. It assumes that we know and embrace ...

- A clear purpose for healthcare
- A clear vision for healthcare
- A shared worldview that reflects the kind of beliefs and convictions necessary for bringing together a wide range of interests in the pursuit of that purpose and vision.

It changes the debate when these are present. It doesn't, however, eliminate the debate, nor should it. Even when we agree on the purpose and vision for healthcare, we may not agree on how to get there. But if we share a common worldview, as we described it above, we will have the kind of healthy and necessary debate that ultimately unveils the best path to pursue that purpose and vision.

When two or more parties are bound by a common purpose and a common vision, when they buy into the same worldview, at least in terms of how they interact, they can form a durable alliance. The problem and challenge in healthcare is that no such common purpose and vision exists, which makes a common focus virtually impossible. We have no common focus on organizing healthcare to pursue that purpose and vision. And we suffer because of it. In their absence, focus just becomes the stubborn pursuit of individual interests and agendas.

Instead, we need a *national* focus for the role of healthcare. We need a shared focus that places the health and healthcare of our citizens at the center. We need a productive and healthy work force. We need to keep our seniors as active as possible. We need to have financial resources to help those who need help. Only then will we get what we all want: high-value healthcare, where the country gets what it is paying for.

The good news is that the kind of purpose and vision we are advocating is gathering momentum. More and more voices are calling for this kind of purpose and vision, and the more these voices are amplified the better. And the more momentum this purpose and vision gather, the greater will be the drive for implementing them with the kind of worldview described above.

And as that purpose and vision become clearer and more widely embraced, animated by a common set of convictions, we will then be able to focus our efforts where they are most needed. We're not there yet, and we don't agree on what to focus on. But that can change ... with the right kind of leadership from the right people.

A High Value on Care for Others

Care for others is not *just* about the patient—though it is definitely about the patient. But it is also about everyone else involved in healthcare. It's about policy makers and regulators caring about healthcare providers, and not mistaking them for the enemy. It's about hospital administrators caring about their medical staff. It's about doctors caring about the nurses and the support staff that make their function possible. And it is, of course, a collective care for the patient.

Caring for others is not about pandering. Just as a patient's ultimate healing may depend on a painful intervention, so every stakeholder's ultimate well-being may depend on swallowing some equally unpleasant medicine. Policy makers will need to think and act differently, and so will regulators. Physicians will need to embrace a different role and learn to operate in a different climate. Hospital administrators will need to undergo a paradigm shift in the role their hospital fills and the purpose it fulfills. Their staff will need to think and act very differently. In every case, the transition and transformation they face will be that much easier if those who lead them genuinely care for them.

Such care requires courage.

Courage

In the previous chapter, we unpacked five ways courage is displayed:

1. The courage to know yourself
2. The courage to put the interests of others ahead of your own
3. The courage to confront others
4. The courage to align the organization to its true direction
5. The courage to draw a moral line in the sand

These apply to all stakeholders, but not to all in the same way. The transformation of healthcare delivery is such a profound and radical enterprise that it will require some courageous introspection on the part of every stakeholder. Everyone will need the courage to look inside and explore the fears and concerns behind the emotions these changes surface. It will take courage to redefine our own roles, and without the courage to know ourselves, we are likely to have a rough ride.

It will take courage for policy makers to put the national interests ahead of their own political aspirations and the more narrow interests of their constituents, though paradoxically, pursuing the national interests may ultimately serve their own and their constituents' interests more effectively.

For every stakeholder, it will take courage to confront both those inside their organization as well as other stakeholders outside their organization. Hospital administrators will need to confront their physicians, physicians will need to confront their administrators, physicians will need to confront each other, policy makers will need to confront colleagues as well as their constituents, and every confrontation will require a high level of courage.

Policy makers and healthcare providers both need to display the courage to align the organization to its true direction. But it will look different in each case. For policy makers, the organization is the overall healthcare delivery system, and they will need to enact the legislation that genuinely empowers the system to pursue the purpose and vision for healthcare delivery. That will take courage. For physicians and hospital systems, it will require immense courage to shift their practice and organization to a very different purpose for healthcare.

Courage needs to be exercised in the context of everything else that precedes it—a shared worldview, a commitment to humility, a common focus, and a commitment to the care of others—if all these are present, courage will indeed be noble and powerful—and transformational.

The (Ideal) Discussion around the Table

Let's assume that none of the stakeholders have left the table, and once these five objects have been unpacked, they study them with relative objectivity. And let's assume that the conversation goes well—that it takes the turns it needs to take, and that they collectively reach the conclusions they need to reach. What does that discussion look like?

Almost immediately, they notice the reinforcing cyclical nature to these qualities (as illustrated in the diagram below). They take encouragement from the fact that if they can start the cycle going, there is a high likelihood that the cycle will reinforce itself.

The Reinforcing Cycle

© 2015 LeaderDevelopment Inc.

As they seek common ground, it doesn't take them long to acknowledge the scope of the problem. No one refutes the fact that the country cannot afford the unfunded liabilities for Medicare and Medicaid looming ahead, and they agree on the absolute necessity of saving precious financial resources by eliminating waste, inappropriate utilization, and medical errors.

The break-through comes when the debate launches into the division of responsibilities—the *who-does-what* debate. They all acknowledge that it's important, even vital, to make a clear distinction between Organizational Leadership and Operational Leadership. Someone refers to the D-Day analogy (discussed back in the Preface), where there was a clear distinction among those who planned the invasion, those who trained the troops to carry out the invasion, the troops themselves who executed the invasion, and all those who provided the logistical support to help the troops accomplish the goals of the invasion. With that analogy in mind, all the representatives reach three fundamental agreements:

1. They agree that it is the leaders of the country who must articulate and propagate the mission and the vision. They must "plan" the invasion, and thus fulfill their Organizational Leadership responsibilities. And without hesitation, all the fingers around the table unanimously point to the policy makers—the leaders of the country, represented at the table with their multiple political persuasions present. And the challenge they give these political leaders—in the form of a pointed question—is this: As policy makers, are their decisions framed by the pursuit of better results at lower costs (which is our definition of high-value care), or are they consciously or unconsciously distracted by special interest groups who want to maximize their own self-interests? An uncomfortable question, but one that generates a productive discussion.

2. They also agree on something else of equal importance. These same policy makers are not the best placed to execute the invasion; they are not on the front lines of healthcare. They are not the troops in this particular war. And with the same alacrity as before, the fingers point unanimously to the providers of healthcare—to the ones who actually

practice medicine and who are actually on the front lines of this battle against inefficacy. Each person around the table, including the providers themselves, affirms that it is the task of the providers to focus on the patients, and for this demanding battle, they are the best and the best-trained troops.

3. The regulators initiate the third agreement. Their question is this: "How are we going to monitor all this?" The debate then turns to the measures of success, and with some animation, it surfaces such measures as:

- Fewer hospital admissions
- No avoidable admissions
- No medical errors
- No avoidable visits to the emergency rooms
- Higher productivity for the population
- Children no longer missing school for chronic medical conditions
- Lower total spending on healthcare, or at least a rate of growth at or below inflation

Up to this point, three critical stakeholders have taken hold of the right stakes, so to speak. But what of the other stakeholders? Maintaining its healthy momentum, the discussion now focuses on how the remaining stakeholders can support these frontline troops. They wonder what kind of Organizational and Operational Leadership each could exercise to align their own work to support the providers. They come up with a list of tasks and responsibilities such as:

- Get the logistics right: figure out how each particular stakeholder can contribute to the system to optimize it (this is quite different from the stakeholders' desire to maximize their own sector).
- Conduct research with a focus on improving value.
- Structure payments to support value.
- Structure IT to support the providers in value-driven decision making
- Free the legal system to provide actionable feedback for quality improvement.

- Create a regulatory environment that does not micromanage, but ties goals and standards to outcomes, safety, service, and spending.

So they then reach a critical conclusion: there needs to be a clear distinction among ...

- Those who set and promote the purpose and vision
- Those who monitor the purpose and vision
- Those who carry out the purpose and vision
- And those who support those who carry out the purpose and vision

This kind of discussion may seem utopian and unrealistic. But could it happen? Yes, it could, and perhaps more easily than we might think. If three of the stakeholders in particular (the policy makers, the regulators and the providers) set the pace for the rest, the others would follow. However, it will require an intentional commitment on the part of these stakeholders to focus on the essence of their role.

And now we are back to our starting point. For this to happen, something critically important is necessary: the kind of character qualities that were placed on the table. But what would that look like in each case? What character qualities would each one need to set the pace and change the debate? That's our next question.

What Character Qualities Are Particularly Important for Policy Makers?

It has been said—with much insight—that great leaders accomplish the impossible, while politicians accomplish the possible. It tells us something about the unique challenges policy makers face as political leaders, and we need to understand these challenges to properly answer the question about which character qualities are most important for them. They are faced with two challenges in particular, one that is an unavoidable function of political life, and the other that has to do more with the recent political climate. It will become obvious which character qualities they need when we grasp the intensity of these challenges.

First, we must understand the nature of politics. Political leaders operate in a very different world from anyone else in the workforce, including, of course, those in healthcare. Every other stakeholder has a boss upstream—doctors and nurses have bosses, hospital administrators, engineers, and IT specialists have bosses. In each case, they answer to a boss above them in the organization's hierarchy. For political leaders, it's different. Their bosses are downstream: they answer to the voters who put them into office. So when they come to Washington, their primary concern is not the interests and demands of their party leaders, but the interests and demands of their electors. Given the choice between complying with the wishes of their electorate and complying with those of their party leadership, whatever the pressure from their party leaders, they have no trouble choosing—their electorate will almost always win. If you are a politician leading fellow politicians, you have a thankless task—it's hard to compete against the demands of your colleagues' electorates.

And elected officials know how ruthless a boss their electorates can be. Dismissal at the next election hangs like the sword of Damocles over their entire tenure. As one European politician put it, "We know what we need to do. We just don't know how to get re-elected once we have done it."

This means that policy makers are compelled to work incredibly hard at keeping their job, which has little to do with the business of government. And as a boss, the electorate is difficult to read. Politicians can't just walk into this particular boss's office and ask them exactly what they meant by their statements. They have to poll, guess, assume, surmise ... and they may get it wrong. Even when they get it right, especially when they come from a safe seat with a very clear mandate, they have to navigate the challenge of being at odds with many others in Washington.

This is the nature of politics, and has always been so. The second challenge is more recent, and it has to do with the current climate of debate.

Since the signing of the American Constitution, the history of political debate has been a history of animated, aggressive, impassioned debate, interspersed with periods of particularly acidic, virulent, and hot-tempered intransigence. We are in such a time today, where the debate is arguably as acidic, virulent, and hot-tempered as it has ever been. And that is particularly challenging to any policy maker who actually wants to get something done and wants to do so with some level of bipartisanship. For many, compromise has become a dirty word, and yet without it, the Declaration of Independence would never have been signed and the Constitution would never have been drafted.

The wonder is that anything gets done at all in this highly charged and challenging climate. And yet it is in this climate that we are asking policy makers to exercise a high level of Organizational Leadership, and to do so by using the packages opened up on the table.

And what would that look like? Which of the character qualities we identified earlier are particularly important for healthcare policy makers? We suggest the following:

1. Courage
2. A focus on the essential
3. A common worldview
4. Humility

Let's take a closer look at each one.

Courage

This is the one that comes to mind first—and for an obvious reason: nothing else matters without it. No wonder Churchill considered this the greatest of all qualities. And policy makers are called to exercise it more than most. It requires inordinate amounts of courage to come to some kind of compromise, especially when the electorates from homogeneous, partisan and virulent districts are looking over their shoulders. The homogeneity of many districts is, by the way, a product of a history of gerrymandering, uncomfortably common in Congress.

But the good news is that it only takes a handful to turn the tide—and sometimes only one. As Andrew Jackson put it, "One man with courage makes a majority." You could well be that one person if you are a policy maker and reading this. And if we were the members of your district, we would do well to support such courage.

When everything conspires against some level of compromise, it takes courage to face the very accusation of acting without courage, of caving to the majority, and of compromising on principle. There are certainly times when conviction requires a courageous stand, but there are also times when finding common ground requires equal courage. As Henry Clay put it:

"All legislation ... is founded upon the principle of mutual concession ... Let him who elevates himself above humanity, above its weaknesses, its infirmities, its wants, its necessities, say, if he pleases, 'I will never compromise.' But let no one who is not above the frailties of our common nature disdain compromise."

President Kennedy put it this way: "The legislator has some responsibility to conciliate those opposing forces within his state and party and to represent them in the larger clash of interests on the national level; and he alone knows that there are few if any issues where all the truth and all the right and all the angels are on one side."[32]

Of the five expressions of courage we have been discussing in this chapter and the previous one, three in particular stand out:

1. The courage to align the organization to its true direction
2. The courage to put the interests of others ahead of your own
3. The courage to confront others

This isn't to say that the other expressions of courage are irrelevant—they are far from irrelevant. Policy makers will often be called to draw a moral line in the sand and to demonstrate a care for others. But for the transformation of healthcare, these three are particularly important.

Why so? It's one thing to define and clarify direction, but it's another to align an organization to that direction, and still another to align a whole sector to a purpose and vision that is gathering widespread endorsement, but is still encountering significant resistance. That requires courage. It requires courage

---

32   John F. Kennedy, *Profiles in Courage*

to create alliances, cajole fellow policy makers, and debate recalcitrant electors, all for the purpose of embracing legislation that reinforces the purpose and vision of healthcare and that frees up the frontline troops to actually execute it. It requires courage to confront those who are putting their own interests ahead of the nation's and those of the patient, which, if they could only see it, are the same as their own.

There are times when national interest takes precedence over local interests. There are issues where collective interests take precedence over partisan interests. Reforming healthcare now is such a time and such an issue.

A Focus on the Essential

Courage comes much more easily if we are clear on the direction we are setting— if we clearly understand and embrace the purpose and vision for healthcare.

The kind of purpose and vision we are proposing—and the kind that is now gathering momentum—makes it that much easier to embrace. In Chapter Five, we defined the purpose of healthcare this way:

> **The purpose of healthcare is to provide the patient**
> **with value—better outcomes at lower cost.**

And we defined the vision of healthcare as follows:

> **The vision for healthcare is high-quality,**
> **affordable healthcare for everyone.**

Of all the packages on the table, this one may be the easiest for policy makers to open and own. Not that it's easy, but the purpose and vision is bipartisan enough that it shouldn't stretch beyond cooperation the particular sensibilities of the different sides of the aisle. The reason they will embrace the components of the purpose and vision will be different—whether driven by social concerns or economic imperatives—but however different the motivation in pursuing the goal, they can still share the goal. Common goals have in the past brought together strange bedfellows, and this might just be one of them.

However, the key is grasping the importance of the purpose and vision. The more they grasp, on both sides of the aisle, their significance and impact, the more passion and energy they will bring to defending and promoting them—whatever their political persuasion.

A Common Worldview and a Commitment to Humility

Policy makers are more likely to buy into a common worldview if they embrace and own the purpose and vision. If policy makers do indeed buy into the purpose and vision, the debate they engage in needs to be framed by a worldview that acknowledges the principles of debate we discussed earlier in the chapter. These include:

- Collaboration is good
- No one has all the answers
- Compromise may produce a better outcome
- Honest, respectful debate is healthy
- Moral standards are important

If the debate on healthcare reform can be "de-moralized;" if policy makers can debate healthcare reform without a partisan filter, the healthcare debate will itself be reformed. And that will happen if there is enough of a commitment to humility that sets aside personal and political agendas in the pursuit of the greater national good.

What Character Qualities Are Particularly Important for Healthcare Providers?

The character qualities that healthcare providers need to exercise are the same as for the other stakeholders—but their expression will look very different. It will certainly make it much easier for providers to display the right character qualities if the policy makers exercise the right kind of Organizational Leadership with the right kind of character qualities ... but what if they don't? If they don't, the providers need to display these character qualities anyway. Tough but doable—and as we shall see in the next chapter, some are doing so already.

So, as the healthcare providers ponder the packages on the table, which ones should they pay particular attention to? We suggest all of them, but in this sequence:

1. Courage
2. A focus on the essentials
3. A common worldview
4. A high value placed on care for others
5. A commitment to humility

Character Quality #1: Courage

Courage for healthcare providers looks very different than for policy makers, but it's no less real, no less important, and definitely no less challenging. To rearrange the five expressions of courage for healthcare providers, here's how we'll address them:

1. The courage to align the organization to its true direction
2. The courage to put the interests of others ahead of your own
3. The courage to confront others
4. The courage to know yourself
5. The courage to draw a moral line in the sand

The courage to align the organization to its true (new) direction. Hospital administrators and physicians in a given geographic area will most likely have some kind of purpose and vision for their contribution to the community they serve. But if they buy into the purpose and vision above, it will force them into a radical paradigm shift. They will have to figure out how to survive financially by keeping people out of their hospitals instead of pulling them in. It will require making tough decisions, letting go of some programs and initiatives, and promoting others—sometimes the ones they let go are income generators and the ones they promote are financially uncertain at best ... *That requires courage.*

The courage to put the interests of others ahead of your own. Physicians typically don't see themselves as leaders. They see themselves as specialists, and they have a hard time assuming the role of making other people successful when their whole focus has been on the success of their own individual contribution. It requires courage to focus less on the expression of their own expertise and more on the expression and development of other people's expertise.

The courage to confront others. Healthy confrontation is a learned skill that healthcare providers are seldom taught. Physicians generally have no difficulty confronting each other, their staff, or their hospital administrators, but usually the confrontation is unhealthy and either openly or passively aggressive. Physicians often compete with each other and their administration. If providers can put the interests of others ahead of their own, they will learn how to engage in healthy confrontation.

The courage to know yourself. One of the cornerstones of healthcare reform is the responsibility healthcare providers assume in leading on the frontlines of this war on inefficiency and ineffectiveness. To fulfill that role, healthcare providers need to understand themselves—how they are wired, what their strengths and weaknesses are, what their deeper aspirations are—in ways they never had to when they were delivering their medical expertise as individual contributors. Great leaders have huge amounts of self-awareness, and that kind of self-awareness requires courage.

The courage to draw a line in the sand. At some point, healthcare providers are confronted with an ethical dilemma that means crossing an ethical line or stopping short of it. Stopping short requires courage.

Character Quality #2: A Focus on the Essentials

Many physicians have no argument with the purpose and vision of healthcare—in fact, they embrace it. It intuitively resonates with them. The purpose and vision are in fact an expression of the Hippocratic Oath, one they quickly recognize. But giving it a head nod is not enough; physicians and all providers need to not only embrace the purpose and vision but also propagate them—

talking them up, measuring performance against them, and viewing all decisions in their light.

For hospital administrators, it's a different story. The purpose and vision may sound good, but they have a hospital to run and bills to pay. For those hospital administrators who do buy into the purpose and vision, it will require a hefty dose of courage to implement it.

Character Quality #3: A Common Worldview

Earlier we identified five critical elements of a common worldview:

- Collaboration is good
- No one has all the answers
- Compromise may produce a better outcome
- Honest, respectful debate is healthy
- Moral standards are important

Few medical systems promote collaboration. Few environments remove the physicians' burden of having all the answers and give them the freedom to invite input. Few engage in honest debate. But those that do actually stand out, as we shall see in the next chapter.

Character Quality #4: A High Value on Care for Others

Caring for the patient is, or should be, a given, even if for some it is a very secondary concern. Beyond the patient, the issue for healthcare providers is the care they demonstrate for the people who work for them. Some cultures in healthcare are highly respectful, and some are not. Generally those that are respectful perform better than those that are not. The research is pretty conclusive, and it tells us that one of the substantial differences in the performance of different organizations is a function of this one fact: the value they place on the people who work for them. Hospitals are no exception.

The fact is that such care is costly. It costs time and effort. And in the pressure to perform in a highly pressured environment, placing a high value on the people who work there gets lost in the urgency.

It takes courage to invest in others. It takes courage to create the culture where people are nurtured and developed.

Character Quality #5: A Commitment to Humility
Humility in leadership is a surprising character quality, but a surprisingly endearing one. It's much easier to follow someone who is more committed to the success of the organization and the success of people working in it than it is to follow someone who is more committed to their own success. The leader who leads with humility focuses on the good of the organization and the good of those working in it. They listen and debate in such a way that everyone can buy into the pursuit of the greater good. Such humility is attractive and contagious, but it's challenging … it requires courage.

What Character Qualities Are Particularly Important for Regulators?

Regulators wield immense power. As we saw in Chapter Five, and as illustrated below, they touch every single domain of healthcare.

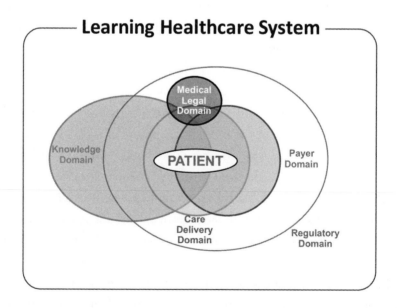

Policy makers may define and enact legislation, but regulators enforce it, and in doing so, they exercise tremendous power. How they use that power is a matter of character. The packages on the table they need to unpack and own, we suggest, are the following:

1. A focus on the essential
2. A common worldview
3. Courage

The others certainly apply—they will need, like everyone else, to place a high value on care for others, and they will need to operate with a high level of humility, but these will more than likely follow if they unpack the other three first.

In many ways, the qualities necessary for regulators are very similar to those for the previous two stakeholders, but at the risk of sounding repetitive, the role of regulators is important enough that we need to address them specifically.

Character Quality #1: A Focus on the Essential

The paradox of authority is that the more responsibility we carry, the more we are tempted to take ownership of processes, not just outcomes. The regulators of healthcare are no exception. With the best of intentions, they are trying to command the troops landing on Omaha Beach from an office somewhere in England. As the enforcers of healthcare standards and practice, they become micromanagers and encroach on a responsibility that doesn't belong to them.

This mission creep is carried out with the best of intentions, and regulators are for the most part animated by a heightened sense of public service. But it is mission creep nonetheless.

The fault lies not with them, but with the absence of a clear purpose and vision. In the absence of such a purpose and vision, outcomes become blurred and indistinct, and regulators inevitably gravitate to what is clear and distinct— the processes of healthcare. In defaulting to regulating processes rather than outcomes, they have unavoidably succumbed to *rewarding* processes rather than outcomes.

In Chapter Three, we introduced you to the SIPOC model, illustrated below, a useful tool that highlights the importance of focusing on outcomes, not processes. In this model, the interests of the customer—the patient and the general population—are defined by the purpose and the vision.

SIPOC Model
The Big Picture

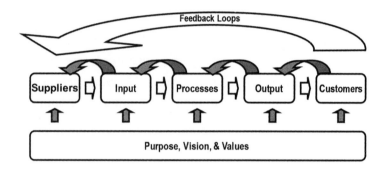

Only when the regulators have a clear sense of purpose and vision can they focus on outcomes—and leave the processes to healthcare providers. It is not the primary job of regulators to regulate processes; it is their primary job to regulate *outcomes*—and to reward and punish the success and failure of outcomes. That can happen only when they have been given a clear sense of purpose and vision—a clear focus on the essentials.

Character Quality #2: A Common Worldview
Because of the power they wield, regulators can influence not only the outcomes of the debate among the different domains, but also the way the debate is conducted. If they embrace the common worldview we defined

earlier, they can change the tone and use their influence to frame the debate in the following terms:

- Collaboration is good
- No one has all the answers
- Compromise may produce a better outcome
- Honest, respectful debate is healthy
- Moral standards are important

If regulators recognize the influence they exert, they can help change the tone of the debate.

Character Quality #3: Courage

Last but not least, courage. Regulators face the constant challenge of trying to reconcile the often irreconcilable tensions among the different domains. They currently do so in a climate of unclear purpose and ill-defined vision. But with a clear purpose and a well-defined vision, they are freed to focus on outcomes, thus fulfilling a critical role in healthcare's relentless pursuit of its purpose and vision. Such a role requires the courage to keep the focus on outcomes, to avoid the temptation of gravitating to processes instead of outcomes, and to confront where confrontation is needed.

Wrap Up

We started this chapter by saying this was perhaps the most important chapter in the book. After reading it, we hope you agree … if these stakeholders don't sit at the table, have the kind of conversation we described, take hold of these packages, unpack them, and use them, there will be no lasting, meaningful reform. Change will inevitably come to healthcare delivery, but without these stakeholders embracing these qualities, it won't be reform, it won't be what it could be, and it will likely be what it shouldn't be.

Can lasting, healthy reform really happen? Can the kind of transformation happen that healthcare needs? Yes, it certainly can, and the proof lies in the multitude of micro examples we see throughout the country … and that's the subject of the next chapter.

PART IV

The Heroes in Healthcare: The Leaders Who Are Doing It Already

This final section is about examples—examples from a small set of medical care delivery organizations, whose leaders exemplify the kind of leadership we have been advocating throughout this book.

These examples illustrate new delivery models, each one driven by a vision for better results at lower cost. They are collected into one chapter because collectively they bring together, to varying degrees and at various levels, the points discussed in all the other chapters of the book.

These are indeed heroes in healthcare.

Chapter 15

Who Are the Success Stories in Healthcare?

I f at this point you have any vestige of doubt about the importance of the leadership prescription laid out in the previous chapters, we bring you one final argument: This prescription actually works! In fact, we have seen it for ourselves.

There are plenty of examples where organizations accomplished precisely what we advocate in these pages, and they have done so on their own initiative—intuitively and creatively, putting one foot in front of the other. In this chapter we highlight eight such examples; organizations that found ways to deliver patient-centered, high-value care, and did so despite the limitations and barriers that currently plague the U.S. healthcare system.

And in every case, leadership was the decisive element or the critical variable. These examples range from integrated systems (such as Advocate) to programs focused on the needs of specific populations (such as MedStar with the frail elderly). In every case, visionary and transformative leadership proved to be the key ingredient to ensure the success of a given initiative or practice redesign.

Each case study begins with an overview of the program or organization (in some cases both) and its journey to high-value care. Each one concludes with a few select leadership lessons. In addition to these leadership highlights, all these case studies demonstrate the following common leadership features:

1. The development of a shared vision
2. A change of culture needed for integration
3. High degrees of collaboration
4. A strong focus on quality while reducing waste
5. An intentional effort to work with or develop a willing payer
6. A clear and ongoing commitment to the goal of keeping people in better health through various forms of prevention.

It is always risky to highlight high performers. We have seen it done in the past, only to witness some then fall to unforeseen market conditions. But whatever the future performance of these case studies, the fact is that they stand today as powerful examples of what can be done. And these eight examples are by no means isolated cases. We have found many other examples of organizations around the country (and around the globe) successfully moving towards this new vision of patient-centered, high-value care.

These examples also highlight something else of critical importance: while some are demonstrating remarkable leadership within the healthcare delivery domain, a similar level of leadership in the other domains is conspicuously absent. The country needs immediate and real leadership from these other domains, in particular from payers, policy makers, and regulators, to help facilitate and ensure the multiplication and scalability of these examples across the nation.

With this in mind, let's take a look at these exciting examples of leadership within healthcare.

1. Advocate Healthcare/Advocate Physician Partners: Clinical Integration Program

Advocate Healthcare and Advocate Physician Partners (APP) created their Clinical Integration Program in 2003 to reduce costs and improve quality by building a culture of learning, collaboration, and value into the system.[33] To accomplish these goals, the Clinical Integration program provides direct support and infrastructure to independent physicians who are members of APP, coupled with a payment model linked to performance that creates the right incentives and alignment to promote superior performance.

There are many challenges associated with organizing independent physicians into a collaborative initiative. As stated by Dr. Lee B. Sacks, Chief Executive Officer of Advocate Physician Partners and Executive Vice President and Chief Medical Officer of Advocate, "We've learned through our experience with APP over the years that infrastructure is the 'secret sauce' that allows clinicians to be a team that can improve care."[34] To that end, Advocate and APP made gradual, yet significant investments in IT infrastructure, and they created protocols and guidelines to support the implementation of best practices by participating physicians.

Early on, Advocate leadership also recognized that the success of their model was highly dependent on a strong physician base. Advocate provides a range of options for physicians who wish to establish affiliation, and provides physicians with ample leadership opportunities throughout the system. This explains why physicians make up half of the seats on governance boards throughout the health system. "This arrangement creates a structure that enables physicians and hospitals to work together to improve care with common quality and cost-effectiveness goals. Physicians and hospitals are collectively accountable for quality and cost during negotiations with payers."[21] Furthermore, having such a strong physician presence in the health system's governance not only ensures physician involvement in the development of pay-for-performance metrics, but also translates to widespread physician acceptance of performance measurement and improvement.

Finally, recognizing the shortcomings of fee-for-service reimbursement, Advocate developed what became known as their style of pay-for-

---

33   Lowrey, Annie. A health provider strives to keep hospital beds empty. *New York Times.* 2013.

34   Pizzo and Grube. 2011. Getting to There from Here: Evolving to ACOs Through Clinical Integration Programs.

performance model, which was tailored to their own practice model. This new payment model bases physician reimbursement on "performance against an extensive list of metrics ... that cover technology use, efficiency, quality, safety, and patient experience."[21] In fact, a given physician's incentive depends not just on their individual performance, but may also depend on the performance of their specialty across the system, within their PHO (Physician-Hospital Organization), and throughout the entire clinically integrated network.

The Clinical Integration Program has shown some striking results across a number of conditions. For example, the asthma initiative resulted in annual cost savings of $16 million compared to national average costs, while screening for depression in patients with diabetes or cardiac conditions resulted in more than $10.8 million annual savings below the costs of standard practice.[23]

Key Leadership Lessons

Communicate a clear vision and strategy. Through systems design, compliance to best practices, and collaboration, Advocate continually seeks to improve quality outcomes for their patients at a low and sustainable cost. The impact of the resulting improved quality extends outside the boundaries of Advocate. As Mark Grube states, "... doctors who practice with Advocate often also practice at other hospitals ... what is occurring is that even when they are practicing at hospitals that are not under value-based contracts, they've changed how they practice. We're seeing declines in utilization there, too."[22]

Create a culture of transparency and teamwork. Advocate publishes an annual Value Report highlighting the actual performance data from its physicians against national and/or industry benchmarks. The report is available to both those within the organization and the public. "The structure of this report helps maintain the partnership's focus on having a business case. By aligning the individual self-interests of key stakeholders, the partnership creates value through collaboration."

Insist on operational excellence. Between 2004 and 2010, Advocate introduced a number of technologies to improve clinical operations. Those practices that did not comply with technology adoption (despite resources provided by APP to help with the transition) were not credentialed by APP for the following year, sending a powerful message to the participating providers.

2. Denver Health: Level One Care for All

Established in 1860, Denver Health and Hospital Authority (DHHA) is now the largest safety-net provider in Colorado and serves approximately one-third of all Denver residents annually. A highly integrated healthcare system, the organization includes the Denver Health Medical Center, with 525 beds for admissions, as well as a large network of community health centers, school-based clinics, health insurance offerings, and other programs touching the lives of millions of people every year. Once a struggling public health system, strong leadership by Dr. Patricia Gabow, the CEO of Denver Health from 1992 through 2012, reorganized it to become a nationally recognized quality healthcare provider. It became a remarkable success story.

However, being a high-value provider has always been a challenge. In the mid-1990s, Denver Health found itself in a particularly tough situation—facing significant fiscal pressures and entwined in the constrictions of the city government—which brought into question the organization's ability to stay true to its mission. Dr. Gabow made the case to the then mayor of Denver to let Denver Health become an independent entity. In January 1997, Denver Health officially began its operations as an independent governmental entity, achieving the operational flexibility that would allow it to remain viable and adapt to the rapidly changing healthcare environment.

Since 1997, Denver Health has continued to reinvent itself and establish a culture of improvement and innovation. In the early to mid-2000s, the system introduced a number of new processes and tools, including "lean," based on the Toyota approach to streamlining operations and reducing waste.[35] Since 2005, integration of "lean" into DHHA operations has resulted in both better patient outcomes (it has, for example, one of the lowest mortality rates among academic health centers) as well as a financial benefit of over $194 million.[36] Denver Health also made significant investments in IT infrastructure, and today the

35 Denver Health: A high performance public healthcare system. Commonwealth Fund, 2007
36 Gabow, PA and PL Goodman, 2015. The Lean Prescription: Powerful Medicine for Our Ailing Healthcare System.

DHHA electronic health record system holds patient records from 1996 forward and is available in real time to any of the patient providers.[37] Finally, recognizing that having the right people on staff was key to its ongoing success, Denver Health also addressed workforce development to ensure that it was recruiting and retaining the best people.

Key Leadership Lessons

Communicate and implement a clear vision and strategy. Denver Health leaders have not only clearly articulated a vision of a high-quality healthcare system for all, but also outlined and implemented a number of strategic initiatives (as described above) in support of this vision. They exercised excellent Organizational Leadership (see Chapter 10), creating and clarifying the organization's direction, aligning its resources to that direction, and selling the vision of that direction to the entire organization.

Promote a culture of operational excellence. It is no surprise that behind this success is great leadership. The now-retired Dr. Patricia Gabow, M.D. is widely credited with promoting high-value care through the introduction and ongoing evaluation of evidence-based protocols and standardization across the entire Denver Health system.[38]

3. Extension for Community Healthcare Outcomes (Project ECHO): Changing the World, Fast!

Treating patients with chronic or complex conditions can be difficult, particularly in rural or underserved areas where access to specialist care is often scarce. Primary care physicians in these areas are often isolated and uncomfortable treating such conditions without the help of specialists. In response to these challenges, Dr. Sanjeev Arora at the University of New Mexico (UNM) Health Sciences Center developed Project ECHO to make "specialized medical knowledge accessible wherever it is needed to save and improve people's lives."[39] What was once a system dependent upon the patient coming to the specialist to receive care

---

37   1860-2010: Denver Health—150 Years of Level One Care for ALL.
38   Denver Health: A high performance public healthcare system. Commonwealth Fund, 2007
39   http://echo.unm.edu/about-echo/our-story/. Accessed June 7, 2015

(sometimes driving 250 miles each way for an appointment) soon became a system designed to take the knowledge of the specialist out to the patient. The principal goal of Project ECHO became forced multiplication, the logarithmic expansion in capacity to deliver best practice care to underserved populations.

To accomplish its goals, Project ECHO creates virtual disease-specific learning networks that give rural primary care physicians access to professional interactions and specialists that would otherwise be unavailable. Through weekly tele-ECHO clinics, primary care physicians throughout the state meet with specialists to review patient panels and receive on-going education specific to their patients. This co-management of cases allows primary care physicians to maintain the responsibility for patients and over time grow more independent in their ability to effectively treat complex diseases.

Since its inception in 2003, with a primary focus around improving the care of patients with Hepatitis C (HCV), the program has been recognized nationally as a model for complex disease management. Project ECHO clinicians report greater knowledge and ability to treat HCV as a result of the program, as well as a greater sense professional satisfaction. Moreover, a cohort study that compared patient outcomes from Project ECHO with those of patients treated at UNM, showed that HCV treatment is just as effective through Project ECHO as within the university setting.[40]

Project ECHO has successfully expanded to multiple other conditions, including rheumatology, diabetes, chronic pain, mental health and substance use disorders, HIV/AIDS, and others. Almost 300 teams across New Mexico are now delivering specialized care through Project ECHO. Additionally, the program has spread to multiple other systems including the Department of Veteran's Affairs, Department of Defense, various university systems throughout the United States, as well as internationally to practices in 10 countries including India and Uruguay. Worldwide, 53 university hubs are connected to more than 2400 clinics for 40 different disease areas or conditions. With its unique approach, Project ECHO significantly expands treatment capacity and reach, leading to better care for more patients.

---

40   Arora et al. 2011. Outcomes of Treatment for Hepatitis C Virus Infection by Primary Care Providers. *N Engl J Med*, 364:2199-2207

Key Leadership Lessons

Communicate a clear vision and strategy. "Our vision of the ECHO team is to improve healthcare for the underserved populations all over the world—and to do it fast."[41] This clarity of purpose allowed Dr. Arora to get the project off the ground by developing institutional alignment within UNM, as well as securing the participation of several rural communities. Dr. Arora and his team developed a model that not only serves the needs of the patients in their home state of New Mexico, but one that could also be reproduced around the world.

Empower the front-line. In contrast to most telemedicine practices, Project ECHO does not focus on a one-to-one, doctor-to-patient methodology. Instead, the program adopts a "one-to-many" concept that builds a learning system where specialists provide knowledge and support to a network of front-line healthcare providers who then directly deliver care. "The reason the ECHO model works is that it fundamentally changes the model for specialty care by de-monopolizing the knowledge that is trapped inside the minds of super-specialists."[42]

Ensure operational excellence. New partners in Project ECHO undergo a one to two-day in-person training session to become familiar with protocols and processes of the program. This includes training providers and nurses in treatments as well the technologies used for team communication. Then, primary care teams are placed into the disease-specific learning networks for weekly meetings with UNM disease specialists as well as other primary care providers across the state. ECHO also trains other university hubs around the world by hosting 3-day trainings to assist with replication of the model around the world.

4. Intermountain Healthcare: Care Management Plus

Good care management can improve patient outcomes and at the same time lower the associated healthcare costs—a fact recognized by Intermountain Healthcare, an integrated nonprofit health system based in Utah. Based on this premise, in 1955 they developed the Diabetes Care Management System (DCMS), a standardized, best-practice driven, and coordinated care

---

41 Arora, Sanjeev. Changing the world, fast: Dr. Sanjeev Arora at TEDxABQ. Retrieved from: http://www.youtube.com/watch?v=lY5nlJxac0g
42 Ibid

plan to improve diabetes control through screenings, preventive services, and patient education.

DCMS has created highly effective inter-professional provider teams that include physicians, nurses, pharmacists, diabetes educators, and computer specialists. The teams are supported by one of the more advanced electronic health records in the industry, which allows the providers to identify and follow a given patient throughout the Intermountain system. Other features of the model include:

- A case manager assigned to each patient to monitor care, provide patient education, and check with patients between office visits.
- Provider notifications of missed patient prescriptions.
- Quarterly reports to providers summarizing patient progress and how a given physician's case management metrics compare to their peers.
- Monthly team meetings to review, analyze, and refine the care management processes.
- Centralized care for diabetic patients, including yearly physical exams, flu vaccinations, and prescription refills, offered through the Diabetes Management Clinic at Utah Valley Regional Medical Center.

The DCMS multi-prong approach to disease management has resulted in significant improvements in patient outcomes. Diabetes patients enrolled in the program showed better control of their blood sugars, with a threefold greater reduction in hemoglobin A1c levels compared with the control group. Their patients also had 15-25 percent fewer long-term complications, 20 percent lower mortality rates, and 24 percent fewer hospitalizations than controls.[43] The model continues to yield positive results and "… it is estimated that if 2 percent of the nation's primary care providers adopted care coordination

---

43   Primary care managers supported by information technology systems improve outcomes; reduce costs for patients with complex conditions. *Agency for Healthcare Research and Quality.* 2008. https://innovations.ahrq.gov/profiles/primary-care-managers-supported-information-technology-systems-improve-outcomes-reduce. Accessed June 9, 2015

programs like Care Management Plus, Medicare could potentially save more than $100 million each year."[44]

Key Leadership Lessons

Align initiatives with organizational mission and vision. Care Management Plus is clearly a direct extension of the organization's mission and vision. Intermountain's mission is to provide excellence in healthcare services to the communities in the region, and it pursues this mission through an emphasis on clinical quality at sustainable costs through their integrated system of care. "Early in Intermountain's history, our trustees committed our organization to becoming better, not bigger. That is still our philosophy today … We continually seek to improve our services and to become 'even better.'"[45]

Develop a culture of operational excellence. One of the cornerstones of Intermountain's philosophy is that clinical providers must play an integral role in the research, development, and implementation of new innovations within its healthcare system. Intermountain's leadership team, supporting the vision of the company's Chief Quality Officer, Dr. Brent James, in fact went further: they sought to *systematize* innovation, and as one observer put it, they "focused on designing an improvement system that would systematize and deploy better-quality outcomes and costs throughout the company and that could 'cut through the advocacy to create a sense of discipline and purposeful focus."[46] Critical to this culture of operational excellence was a commitment to empowering the front lines, driven by a senior leadership committed to empowering them.

Think big but start small. Instead of focusing on their entire population of patients with chronic conditions, Intermountain began by focusing attention on only those with diabetes. This clearly defined their patient population to a manageable group and allowed for any adaptations and tailoring to the program to be implemented before it was expanded into Care Management Plus.

---

44 Ibid
45 Baker, G.R. et al. "Intermountain healthcare." *High performing healthcare systems: delivering quality by design*, 2008. Toronto: Longwoods Publishing. 151-178.
46 Ibid

5. Iora Health: Redefining Primary Care

The fragmented nature of the American healthcare system can often be difficult for patients to navigate. This problem is even more difficult for patients with multiple chronic conditions, who must chart a path through various specialists with little to no coordination with their primary care provider.

This was the challenge addressed by Dr. Rushika Fernandopulle who sought to fundamentally change the current system by establishing a new model of care from the ground up. In 2011, after initial success with his Special Care Clinic in Atlantic City and Seattle, Fernandopulle (along with Christopher McKown) co-founded Iora Health—a team-based primary care model.

Patient-centeredness is at the core of Iora's mission, as exemplified by the three key features of its practice model: Team-based care, financial capitation, and a proprietary IT infrastructure. Iora's healthcare "teams" include a primary care physician, nurse, and a health coach, who serves as the primary point of contact for the patient. Coordination and communication surrounding patient's needs are the responsibility of each team member. Morning 'huddles' are conducted each day to review the patient panel and identify those in need of follow up.

Recognizing that incentives built into the current fee-for-service environment do little to produce better outcomes for patients, Iora Health focuses on patient outcomes through financial capitation. The flat, per-member monthly fee frees the clinic from billing responsibilities associated with the fee-for-service model, which not only reduces administrative costs but also allows the providers to do what is best for each patient, even if no billing code for a given service exists.[47]

Finally, Iora's practice is supported by a proprietary IT platform that combines claims, administrative, and clinical data to better serve patients. The system "provides timely updates on patient clinical status, gathered from local hospital census data and pharmaceutical alerts. A list of outstanding clinical and care management tasks keeps the care team aware of and accountable for meeting patient needs."[48] The system is also available to patients online, who are

47   Alspach, Kyle. Iora Health opens Boston-area primary care practice, aiming for innovation in healthcare. Biz Journals, 2013. Retrieved from: http://www.bizjournals.com/boston / blog/startups/2013/03/iora-health-opens-boston-area-primary.html?page=all. Accessed on Sept 26, 2014

48   Jonas, Cabell. Iora Health on Dr. Zubin 'ZDoggMD' Damania's new clinic. *The Advisory Board Company.* 2013. Retrieved from: http://www.advisory.com /research/care-

encouraged to participate in their care and treatment plans, and even add their own notes into their electronic health records.

Iora's approach has shown significant improvements in patient outcomes. When compared to the national average, Iora's patients show better control of hypertension (83 percent vs. 63 percent) and diabetes (85 percent vs. 72 percent).[49] Perhaps it is not surprising that in its first three years, Iora grew to over 10 practices across 7 states, a growth rate they intend to sustain.

Key Leadership Lessons

Communicate a clear vision and strategy. The co-founder of Iora Health, Dr. Rushika Fernandopulle, exemplifies what it means to be a true patient advocate. Through ingenious foresight and a vision to transform healthcare, Fernandopulle clearly established himself as one of the nation's most courageous healthcare leaders. By focusing on the most expensive subsets of patients and an increased investment in primary care, Iora's vision is to create a system that enables patients to better control and navigate their own health, all while lowering overall healthcare costs.

Hire and develop the right people. Starting from scratch has enabled Iora to build the right team, one member at a time—all of who share the Iora vision and a passion to transform healthcare delivery and improve the healthcare experience for patients. Iora tends to hire for personality and cultural fit, rather than a specific skill set. This is particularly true in the case of health coaches, who are the heart of the Iora model.

Create a culture of empowerment. Although some elements of the Iora model (such as the use of the proprietary IT system and the daily huddle) are non-negotiable, each practice is encouraged to adapt its services and offerings to local conditions. Staffs are also provided with flexibility and a small per-patient budget to develop individualized interventions that promote patient adherence to the course of treatment.

---

transformation-center/care-transformation-center-blog/2013/06/iora-health-on-zdoggmd. Accessed on: Sept. 26, 2014

49   http://www.iorahealth.com/real-results/ Accessed June 7, 2015

6. MedStar Total Elder Care (TEC): Value-Based Care for a Complex Population

The healthcare landscape in the United States is undergoing a profound transition, moving away from volume to value-based healthcare. Interestingly, MedStar Washington Hospital Center (MWHC), which serves the greater D.C. area, has been running a value-centric healthcare program since 1999.[50] This home-based primary care model (HBPC), known as MedStar Total Elder Care (TEC), is a mobile care intervention that provides a "single, comprehensive source of home-based medical and social services for frail elders and their families."[51]

Based within the Geriatrics Division of MWHC, the program is the brainchild of two geriatricians, Drs. Eric DeJonge and George Taler. The two physicians recognized that a growing population of elders with severe chronic illness was struggling to find healthcare that successfully addressed all of their medical and social needs.

To better serve the medical and social needs of a complex subgroup of elders, TEC employs mobile, inter-professional teams consisting of geriatricians, nurse practitioners, social workers, licensed practical nurses, and office coordinators. Each team is responsible for building an intimate relationship with a panel of 300 patients and families to help them manage all the ups and downs in the final years of life.

Core TEC services include home-based primary care, 24/7 on-call medical staff, physician continuity to the hospital, intensive social services, and coordination of needed specialty and ancillary services. Care coordination and a strong social work component are keys to the success of the model because many of the TEC patients come from low-income families, which makes over 40 percent of them eligible for both Medicare and Medicaid. In addition, they have multiple chronic conditions (such as diabetes, congestive heart failure, and dementia) and physical disability, which increases their need for intensive medical and social services.

---

50   De Jonge et al. 2014. Effects of Home-Based Primary Care on Medicare Costs in High-Risk Elders. *JAGS*, 62:1825–1831
51   De Jonge et al. 2014 "MedStar Total Elder Care (TEC) Business Plan." MedStar Health.

Weekly all-hands-on-board huddles allow the teams to review, analyze, discuss, and systematically address any issues that come up with individual patients. A mobile electronic health record that allows for live access to patient records (both inpatient and out-patient data), as well as home-based diagnostic tools further supports the teams.

Since its inception, the model has served over 3,100 elders with a current active census of 620 patients. Most referrals into the program are done by word-of-mouth, not surprising given TEC's track record of better patient experience. Moreover, a comparison of TEC patient outcomes and costs with a matched set of controls showed that TEC patients have similar survival outcomes at a 17 percent lower cost than control elders.[52]

Key Leadership Lessons

Communicate a clear vision and strategy. Since its inception in 1999, the program has never deviated from its focus on improving the health and experience of the frail elders and their families. This clarity of vision and the constant focus on "doing the right thing for the right patients at the right time" are some of the reasons TEC has enjoyed the dedicated support of MedStar's leadership, despite the fact that Medstar's traditional financial model as a hospital-based organization (driving higher volumes of admissions) conflicts directly with the goals of TEC—which is *reducing* hospital and ER utilization.

Empower the front line. Although the initial evaluation of patients, 24/7 on-call coverage, and hospital duties are carried out by physicians, continuous patient oversight is the purview of NPs and social workers, who determine the frequency of visits based on medical and social needs. The TEC healthcare professionals experience a deep sense of satisfaction and demonstrate a long-term commitment to the mission of the program. Staff turnover has been very low, with most staff tenure at 5-10 years.

---

52 De Jonge et al. 2014. Effects of Home-Based Primary Care on Medicare Costs in High-Risk Elders. *JAGS*, 62:1825–1831

7. North Texas Specialty Physicians: Improving Population Health Through Teamwork And Information Technology

Established in 1995, North Texas Specialty Physicians (NTSP) is an independent physician association (IPA) that includes more than 900 primary care and specialty physicians. The target market consists of the residents of Tarrant, Johnson, Dallas and Parker counties in North Texas.

All full-member physicians in NTSP pay a fee to join, and they elect representatives to serve on the IPA Board of Directors. In turn, NTPS provides a variety of business and clinical services and tools to its members to support the delivery of high-value, patient-centered healthcare to more than 15,000 patients every day.[53]

NTSP aims "to create and manage superior healthcare models that enable physicians to best serve patients while maintaining their independence."[54] To achieve this vision, NTSP has evolved its strategy to include a value-based physician payment model and an IT infrastructure that not only allows data sharing, but also supports improvements in medical decision making and care management.

NTSP capitates physician services based on specialty. Primary care physicians are paid a capitated fee that increases with improved performance and quality. Specialist physicians receive fee-for-service (FFS) payments for the care they deliver, adjusted monthly to meet budgets for their specialties. At the end of that year, the physician may receive a bonus and distribution based on meeting the division's capitation, efficiency, and quality metrics. By linking a significant portion of the physician's payment to both quality and cost metrics, NTSP physicians have an incentive to avoid over-utilization, and at the same time ensure that patients receive the necessary care.

In 2005, after many board discussions and the realization that better clinical decisions could be achieved by offering more information at the point of care, NTSP decided to make a significant investment (over $10 million) to develop an interoperable health information exchange (HIE). Rather than relying on a

---

53   http://www.ntsp.com/about-ntsp/. Accessed June 14, 2015
54   http://www.ntsp.com/mission-vision/. Accessed June 14, 2015

third-party vendor for HIE development, NTSP decided to design, build, and implement the HIE in-house. In choosing this route, NTSP was able to ensure that every feature and function of the software was focused on providing the necessary information in a logical manner for physicians before, during, and after their visits with the patient.

HIE implementation has resulted in a number of improvements in both the effectiveness and efficiency of care. Colorectal cancer screenings, for example, targeted for appropriate patients, improved from 40 percent to 82 percent over three years, while surgery for colorectal cancer decreased by 30 percent.

Key Leadership Lessons

Establish true physician leadership. In addition to the Board of physicians (with authority and responsibility for the entire clinical practice), a "Division Chair" is selected for each specialty, and this individual is responsible for overseeing the physicians in that specialty and serving as a liaison for the group to the Board.

Create a culture of transparency. Each Division Chair receives quarterly physician specific data on quality, per patient resource use, per patient cost, and patient satisfaction. The data elements are presented to each physician in an un-blinded manner, with peer pressure serving as a strong motivator for improvement.

Create incentives for participation and buy-in. The IPA has always been upfront with its expectations for member participation and conduct. Physicians who do not wish to practice in a manner consistent with the mission and vision of the IPA are encouraged to seek other organizations.

Empower the front line. In addition to the HIE (now commercially available under the name *Sandlot*), NTSP providers are supported by a variety of internal services (such as case and disease management) to create individualized care plans for patients.

8. Virginia Mason Medical Center: Marketplace Collaboratives

In 2004, four large self-insured employers in the Seattle area approached Virginia Mason Medical Center (VMMC) looking for a solution to rising healthcare costs. Recognizing an opportunity to apply the Toyota-based lean delivery model implemented at VMMC two years prior (known as the Virginia Mason Production System), the organization decided to establish what is now known as the Marketplace Collaboratives in which VMMC providers interact directly with employers and their health plan. The aim of each collaboration is to improve the value of healthcare delivery, reducing costs to the provider and to the purchaser, and improving access for patients. Employers select clinical conditions of highest priority, set purchasing standards, and review medical evidence with VMMC providers. Using this customer input, combined with the application of lean management, Dr. Robert Mecklenburg and his colleagues developed and implemented a series of new clinical care models focused on these high-cost conditions—high-cost to both the patients and the payer (in this case the employer of these people). This initiative was strongly reinforced by the visionary support of their CEO, Dr. Gary Kaplan.

It became a great example of effective collaboration among different stakeholders. The initial collaborative set up in 2005 was composed of representatives from VMMC, the four large self-insured employers, and Aetna, their health plan. Starbucks identified low back pain as a significant problem that resulted in high healthcare costs and loss of productivity. Through further analysis of claims data, the VMMC team, led by Dr. Mecklenburg, discovered that 80-85 percent of patients with back pain suffered from uncomplicated conditions easily treated with physical therapy. Moreover, it was determined that 90 percent of the old evaluation and treatment process was absolutely no help at all in treating these patients and getting them back to work. These observations resulted in a radical redesign of the treatment plan for patients with uncomplicated back pain.

In just three months, the back pain collaborative resulted in substantial improvements in patient outcomes (94 percent of patients returned to work the same day, or the day after) and in access to care (the waiting period for an appointment went from 31 days to same-day access), all the while reducing overall treatment costs (from 5 percent above the national average to 9 percent below).[55,56] Building on the success of the back pain collaboration, VMMC

---

55 Ibid
56 Kenney, Charles. Better, faster, more affordable: how Virginia Mason Medical Center took a common complaint and delivered uncommon healthcare. *Seattle Business Magazine.* 2011.

has expanded its Marketplace Collaborations to address a total of 15 high-cost diagnoses, including headache, large joint pain, breast masses, and acute respiratory infection—all with improved results, better access, and lower costs.

The marketplace collaborative model has been scaled and transported beyond Virginia Mason. Beginning in 2009, Virginia Mason assisted the private sector employer Intel in successfully applying the marketplace collaborative model in the Portland, Oregon market.[57] In 2011, the State of Washington as a public sector employer began using a marketplace collaborative, the Robert Bree Collaborative,[58] to set purchasing standards based on quality for high-cost conditions.

Key Leadership Lessons

Clarify the mission and vision, sell the goals, and align the staff. The CEO, Gary Kaplan, MD reset the direction for Virginia Mason when he established the importance for all the staff to focus on the customer. The customer was always the patient, but in many situations they found that an additional key customer was the payer, and the payer ultimately was the patient's employer.

Engage the customer. VMMC included the actual payer—the employer—in collaborative development of both new models of care and new models of payment. Success depended on making these models acceptable to both parties. And it was successful: the payment was linked to the value generated by Virginia Mason for the employer and the patient.

Ensure operational excellence. The foundation for Marketplace Collaboratives was established in 2001 when Dr. Gary Kaplan, as the CEO of VMMC, led his team in efforts to learn and apply lean methodologies designed to identify and eliminate waste within the Virginia Mason system.[59] These efforts inspired and challenged VMMC physicians to question the status quo and to drive further improvements in their delivery of patient care.

Retrieved from: http://www.seattlebusinessmag.com/article/better-faster-more-affordable. Accessed on: Sept. 30, 2014

57 McDonald, Mecklenburg, and Martin, "The Employer-Led Healthcare Revolution," Harvard Business Review, July-August, 2015

58 breecollaborative.org

59 Bisognano M and C Kenney. Pursuing the Triple Aim: Seven Innovators Show The Way To Better Care, Better Health, And Lower Costs. San Francisco: Jossey-Bass. 2012.

Empower the front line. Gary Kaplan ensured that the entire staff was trained in "lean" management and in the Toyota model of workflow process and quality improvement, all the time reducing waste. The organizational leadership assured that these principles were applied to good use by his operational leadership team, which included Dr. Mecklenburg.

Conclusions

If there is one over-arching lesson from these examples, it is that such patient-centered high-value care *is* possible—even with the highly dysfunctional current U.S. healthcare system. And if there is a corollary, it is that these examples exist because leaders made them exist. Leadership really *does* matter!

But at the same time, these examples highlight something else of critical importance: we can and should do so much more at the national level to support such innovations.

- Above all, we need to find ways to improve the interactions among the five domains of the healthcare system and address the major barriers faced by these and other healthcare delivery organizations. Of these critical interactions, those between the care domain on the one hand and the payer and the regulatory domains on the other are especially critical.

- The payer domain needs to move away from the current fee-for-service structure that not only promotes volume over value, but also penalizes the highest-value providers. Payers should work to develop contracting strategies that align incentives and payments with value (better quality at lower costs) across the care continuum. In the absence of a significant shift in provider reimbursement, organizations and initiatives that aim to provide high-value care are at risk of slowly withering away.

- In turn, the regulatory domain must focus on providing oversight to, rather than micromanagement of, the care domain. Specifically, the government must take the lead in requiring transparency of healthcare outcomes, safety, service and cost. They need to ensure and facilitate the transformation of the healthcare system into a learning system. A key step forward would be to require both connectivity and interoperability of information technology systems.

- Finally, the care domain itself must take a critical look inward and ensure that organizational structures, governance, and incentives are aligned with the organization's overarching vision of high value, patient-centred care.

High-value, patient-centred care is not only realistic, but also achievable. However, it will take a strong alignment among government agencies, policy makers, payers, and providers. Without this alignment, we will continue to see only occasional, one-off examples of high-value delivery organizations, led and driven by intrinsically motivated professionals ... instead of such organizations operating out of a much larger, coordinated strategy that brings us to high-value healthcare ... and finally gets us to the point where we are actually "getting what we are paying for!"

Conclusion

Congratulations! If you have made it to this point, you are clearly committed to making a difference in healthcare.

And now you can. Many are worried about healthcare, and they have every reason to be. Its escalating costs and rampant inefficiencies affect us all, either directly or indirectly. But you now have something to hold onto that can really make a difference. We have given you a roadmap and a compass to help you exercise the kind of leadership that can profoundly transform healthcare. Please use these valuable tools to be a difference maker! Whatever your role as a stakeholder, please step up to fulfill the kind of leadership your role requires ... and the kind of leadership that will help to salvage a broken healthcare system within our nation.

And if you are not a stakeholder, but rather, a concerned citizen and a current or future patient—as we all are—please expect and demand from all the stakeholders in healthcare the kind of leadership that you read about in these pages. And as you do, you will be exercising the kind of influence and leadership that our democratic system mandates.

William Faulkner once made a comparison between monuments and footprints. Footprints, he argued, are better than monuments. Monuments tell us that we got so far, and no further. Footprints, on the other hand, tell us that we kept on moving.

The history of healthcare has plenty of monuments, and its own share of monstrosities. Either way, our task is to keep moving, to keep making footprints. But in which direction do we make those footprints? Our hope is that this book has given you the answer.

As you make your footprints, may your impact be profound. And as you keep moving forward, you will find others stepping in beside you. So never stop putting one foot in front of the other!

It is the only way real change will happen. It is the only way we can rescue healthcare.

About the Authors

Antony Bell is founder/CEO of Leader Development Inc., an organization that has helped many leaders in multiple sectors engineer the transformation of their leadership—and through it, the transformation of their organization. He has created an integrated, comprehensive leadership framework that makes sense of the complexities of leadership and brings together all the multiple elements of leadership into a coherent whole. This framework, applicable to any context at any stage of a leader's career, is now widely applied by numerous individuals, consulting companies, coaching companies, government agencies, businesses, and non-profit organizations; it is widely considered the most comprehensive summary of the key elements of great leadership. He is the author of *Great Leadership: What It Is and What It Takes in a Complex World*, and a frequent contributor to the business and leadership press.

For information about the programs and consulting services offered by Leader Development Inc. please contact Antony Bell directly as below:

Work phone: 803 748 1005

Email: abell@leaderdevelopmentinc.com

Denis A. Cortese M.D. practiced medicine, and participated in education, research, and administration at Mayo Clinic for 40 years. In the years prior to retirement from Mayo Clinic in November of 2009 he served as President and CEO of the Mayo Clinic. He currently is a Foundation Professor and Director of the Healthcare Delivery and Policy Program at Arizona State University, and President of the Healthcare Transformation Institute. The goal of these programs is to act as a catalyst for changing healthcare into a high value learning system. The work involves teaching future leaders at undergraduate, graduate, and post-graduate levels and thought direct interactions with leaders of over 40 delivery organizations in the USA, Europe, and Asia. As a member of the National Academy of Medicine, he was the first chair the Roundtable on Value and Science-Driven Medicine (creating under his tenure the *Learning Health System Series*). He is an honorary member of the Royal College of Physicians (UK) and of the Academia Nacional de Medicina (Mexico). Recently publications include the Roadmap Series (*A Roadmap to Better Health, A Roadmap to High-Value Healthcare Delivery*, and *A Roadmap to Medicare Sustainability*), and a chapter titled High-Value Healthcare For All: Innovative Approaches in the United States and The Netherlands, in the book *Breakthrough: From Innovation to Impact,* first edition, Owls Foundation, The Netherlands.

Contact information:

Cell Phone: 602 451 4322

Email: denis.cortese@asu.edu or cortese.denis@mayo.edu

A free eBook edition is available with the purchase of this book.

To claim your free eBook edition:

1. Download the Shelfie app.
2. Write your name in upper case in the box.
3. Use the Shelfie app to submit a photo.
4. Download your eBook to any device.

Shelfie

A free eBook edition is available
with the purchase of this print book.

CLEARLY PRINT YOUR NAME ABOVE IN UPPER CASE

Instructions to claim your free eBook edition:
1. Download the Shelfie app for Android or iOS
2. Write your name in **UPPER CASE** above
3. Use the Shelfie app to submit a photo
4. Download your eBook to any device

Print & Digital Together Forever.

Snap a photo

Free eBook

Read anywhere

The Morgan James Speakers Group

↗ www.TheMorganJamesSpeakersGroup.com

We connect Morgan James published authors with live and online events and audiences whom will benefit from their expertise.